John Gallagher

The World's Best Rugby Player ?

With Chris Brown
Alan McColm

R&B Publishing

R&B Publishing
P.O.Box 200
Harrogate
HG2 9RB
England

First published 1991

British Library Cataloguing in Publication Data

Brown, Chris
John Gallagher : the world's best rugby player.
I. Title II. McColm, Alan
796.333092

ISBN 1-873668-50-3

Typeset by R&B Publishing, Harrogate
Printed and bound in Great Britain by Mackays of Chatham Plc.

Contents

Chapter 1

The Milk Round

"John Gallagher from Two-South. Report to Brother John's office immediately" crackled over the aged school tannoy, barely fifteen minutes into the first lesson of the week. There was no mistaking the dulcet tones of Brother John's own northern accent. I didn't know from how far north or from which county he came, but I knew he wasn't a southerner. At the tender age of twelve, and having lived all my life in London, anything beyond Watford was 'The North' to me.

The lads from the rugby team, including my friend Kieran Masterson, had already cornered me.

"Where the hell were you on Saturday ?"

"Why ?" I asked.

"Bob Bacon wasn't very happy with you."

"Oh, it'll be alright. I only missed a game of rugby !"

Now they were all turned round looking at me with 'We told you so' smirked right across their faces.

St Joseph's Academy was one of the original Grammar Schools, not a fee-paying school but one with entry obtained by passing the eleven-plus exam. Being a traditional 'De La Salle' Catholic school most of the teachers were known as 'Brother'. It was also a traditional Rugby Union school with no soccer being played at all. This had annoyed me at the time because I was soccer-mad, a keen Arsenal supporter and I just loved playing the game. I had been captain of my primary school team and scored 31 goals in my final year. With academy school rugby being played on a Saturday, that only left me with Sunday to get soccer out of my system.

Early in my second year at St Joseph's Academy I was offered a milk round for £6 a day, including tips, which was very good money. My elder brother, Mike, and all my friends were already earning some extra pocket money with week-end jobs, and I wanted to join them. The round was on Saturdays which didn't bother me because I could still play soccer on Sundays, so I decided to accept. I'd duly started work the next week and missed a school rugby game against the neighbouring school.

Miss Farrar, our second year history teacher, was glaring straight at me. She was stood in front of the blackboard having stopped making notes about The Armada in mid-sentence; "It sounds like the head-master means you John. Don't you think you should run along ?" she said. I knew then that I was in real trouble.

As I approached Brother John's office I was thinking 'Crikey, here we go, the third degree'. I had only been in his office once before and that was for my interview when I first came to the school. The only other thing I knew was that all the 'beatings' took place in there. I certainly wasn't going to get a pat on the back. I knocked and entered the office. The headmaster, Brother John, was sitting behind his huge old desk with Mr Bacon, our games master, at one corner.

It was Brother John who did all the talking: "Now young Master Gallagher, I hear you missed the rugby game last Saturday. Is that correct ?," he boomed. "Yes, Sir," I replied, looking intently at the deep-pile blue carpet. Hearing my reply, Brother John proceeded to give me a not-so-short lecture on the school's tradition of rugby and how long they had been playing it, which was longer than the game had been invented if my memory serves me right. After what seemed like ages he had exhausted himself and I was asked for my reasons for not playing. I replied, "I've started a milk round".

This answer only seemed to make things worse. He told me that he knew both of my parents, knew they both worked and knew we were not on the poverty line. Was there any reason they should send their son out to work at such a young age ? I proudly replied that it had been my sole decision.

"Well, Master Gallagher, you have two choices," decided Brother John, "Either you give up this milk round, which you don't really need, and turn up for training with Mr Bacon tomorrow. Or you can continue with your milk round and find yourself another school !". I was devastated; at the age of twelve my future had just been chosen for me.

My mother, Ann, is Irish and had come over to London with her brother, Michael, from Limerick when she was only eighteen. She had made the journey partly to find work as a nurse and partly to escape the confines of her large family. My father, Sean, is also Irish, from Derry but went over to Malaya with his family when he was eight years old because my Grandfather was in the army. The family returned to England when he was around fourteen.

I was born at teatime on the 29th January 1964 at home in Ladywell, south-east London. My elder brother Mike had been born two years previously and my younger brother, Pat, was born five years later. Ann, Sean, Michael, John and Patrick - a good Irish family ! Ladywell is a small residential area in Lewisham, sandwiched between New Cross, Brockley and Catford. We lived in a small two-story terraced house in a road running parallel to the local railway track. At the end of the road was a river, affectionately known as the River Quaggy, with a concrete bridge over to the local park where I spent a lot of my childhood pretending to be Bobby Charlton.

My early days were very happy and, like those of most kids at the time, they were dominated by football. England had just won the World Cup and football was on TV a lot of the time. By playing it ourselves, we were emulating our heroes and the 'bigger boys' of the area. I used to knock around with a gang of about ten or eleven boys from our back street with an age range of about two years. The gang included my older brother Mike but not Pat because he was always too young. Every day we used to play football in the park or the street. The only times we ever stopped were to watch the matches on TV.

In 1970 I became a Chelsea supporter when they won the FA Cup. It wasn't just their victory which made me pledge my everlasting allegiance it was also the fact that I liked the colour of their shirts. As a full-blooded disciple I started collecting posters of the team and plastered them all round my room at home. I even asked Mum to buy me a Chelsea top for my birthday.

A year later, Arsenal won The Cup and I swapped allegiance to them. All of the Chelsea pictures came down to be replaced by ones of Arsenal. With a new shirt, the transformation was complete and nobody would have ever known I'd even heard of Stamford Bridge. The same would have happened the following year when Leeds beat Arsenal in the 1972 Cup. However, by then I'd decided it was time to 'settle down' and I have remained a Gunners fan ever since.

We were, and continue to be, a very close and loving family. Mum was great and used to run the show at home, always keeping things ticking over, cooking, cleaning, looking after us boys and also going out to work as a nurse. My father, as in most households, was used as a bit of a threat to keep us three rowdy boys in check. An occasional whack with the back of the hand and banishment up to our respective rooms would make sure that we didn't over step the mark.

Dad worked in the Metropolitan Police and spent a period in the C.I.D. He used to have to put in long hours on shift, sometimes fourteen or fifteen hours. However, we always saw plenty of him, and he used to play football with us or take us to the local swimming baths for a treat. On one occasion he took us to the Catford Dog Track, to see the police dogs pretending to catch villains and rip their arms off - great stuff for young boys.

One of my mother's sisters called Noreen also lived in our house for a few years. She was given the unenviable task of babysitting for Mike, Pat and me, enabling Mum to go back to work. With Mum working shifts as a nurse and Dad working shifts in the police, there were some occasions when they both had to work at the same time. Noreen was only fifteen years older than me which meant that our relationship formed as if she were somewhere between an older sister and a second mother.

While Noreen was in the house, Mike and I shared a bedroom. He used to take full advantage of the situation to scare the wits out of me. I would regularly jump into bed and find a huge mock spider or something else that he had hidden in there. Once I was snuggled down and starting to dose-off, he would use pieces of cotton which he'd tied to the bed sheets to slowly pull the covers off me. Other pieces would be used to make the wardrobe doors creek open and shut until I screamed and jumped out of bed to switch on the lights, much to his amusement. The stories that he would tell me as I was trying to get back to sleep used to have me trembling. I'll say one thing for Mike, he had a hell of an imagination even at that age.

When we got older, I was about eleven, Mike was about thirteen, Mum and Dad would sometimes go out and leave us without an adult in the house. The living room was instantly transformed with a corner of the TV forming one goal post and an edge of the settee the other. We would then whack my deflated leather ball around the house after we'd given it a clean. Several FA Cup matches and World Cup finals were decided in this way. Although we used to hide any ornaments or small objects that could be broken, we had more than a few close calls with the windows. I'm sure that my parents would have had a fit if they'd ever found out.

On another occasion when we were left alone the Winter Olympics were on the TV. To join in we used the staircase as a toboggan run with our sleeping bags as the toboggans. It was a bit tight coming down side-by-side and we got lots of bumps and bruises on our elbows when we smacked the bannisters.

Being fairly competitive we organised a knock out competition where we both represented a variety of international bobsleigh teams. All of the practice runs and preliminary rounds were completed before the big final. By pure luck it was the two British sleds which had reached the final. Mike was in Great Britain-1 and I was in Great Britain-A because we couldn't agree who should be in the 'first' sled and who should be in the 'second'.

The race for the Gold Medal was very close with elbows flying in all directions. Just five short steps from the bottom, I started to get a bit of a lead over Mike and prematurely started to celebrate. However, I had underestimated how badly he wanted to win. Somehow Mike managed to stick out his ankle so that I went flying head-first through the bottom glass panel of the front door. It could have been very nasty but luckily I only ended up with a small cut on my finger.

Chapter 2

A Different Ball Game

I started going to St Joseph's Academy at the age of eleven. Mike had been there for a couple of years and all of my friends from primary school were heading in that direction, so naturally I wanted to join them. I knew that the school played rugby rather than football but I wanted to remain part of the gang.

All first years were taken to the sports hall changing rooms on the first Wednesday and given one of four different coloured jerseys indicating which 'house' they were in. There was St David's, St George's, De La Salle and I was in St Patrick's who played in, believe it or not, green jerseys.

We were then marched out onto the junior rugby pitches and an oval ball was thrown up in the air. One lad who had seen the game before picked up the ball and started running. Nobody else really knew what to do but we got the idea that we should stop him somehow. The ball carrier set off on one of those runs which is a signature of children's rugby - the across pitch sprint - making very little headway. When everybody caught him up, he just disappeared under a pile of bodies.

Our tackling was to remain much the same for most of the first year, using numbers rather than skill. The fact that the ball ever came out of the pile of bodies was amazing. When it did, it always rolled around on the ground for several seconds as we tried to pick it up. The teachers obviously didn't care too much about 'knocking-on'.

One of my friends, Martin Quin or Quinny, usually ended up with the ball. He was one of those early developers who looked fully grown by the age of ten. Since he was about four foot taller than the rest of us (and I think he had a moustache by then) not many of us could argue with him on the pitch. Unfortunately he wasn't on my side.

The first-year school rugby team was picked half way through the first term, in late October. I found myself playing at stand-off, possibly because of my relatively small size. Quinny was picked as the No.8. In the first few games, he simply used to pick the ball out of the base of the scrum and use his size to run forward for a try. As a result I didn't get to see much of the ball.

Our third or fourth game was against Eaglesfield School and, as usual, I found myself running alongside Quinny who had the ball. Only needing to beat the opposition's full-back, who was even smaller than me, another try looked certain. The last thing I expected was for him to pass the ball. He did and I dropped it right in front of the try line. Quinny was furious and vowed never to pass the ball to me again. Luckily, he had a lapse in concentration about five minutes later and he gave me another pass. This time I held on and scored my first ever try.

I went home and told my Mum what I had done. Being used to only hearing about all the goals that I had scored, she turned round and asked, "What's a try ?". My reply was, "I don't know, but I got one !".

Quinny continued to dominate our games until we got a new coach at the end of the second year. Although the rest of the team was happy with him scoring all the tries and kicking all the goals (we didn't care so long as we were winning), the new coach took a different view and dropped him from the team. When he was re-instated, he had learned how to pass a bit more frequently.

For some reason I got it into my thick head that I couldn't wear soccer boots for rugby. I'd decided that I needed a pair of big high-cut boots with steel toe-caps. Mum managed to get a pair for me from a lad down the road who had just finished at St Joe's. They were two odd boots and hadn't been worn for years but they were in my size; big, old, heavy things with the studs on one of the boots being nailed in and the other's being made from moulded rubber. I played in them for a couple of weeks but kept coming home with huge blood blisters.

One day I said to my Mum "Look these are useless" pointing to my sore toes. They must have been bad because she took me straight down the shops to buy a new pair. Still having the same opinions about which boots I needed, I got a pair of high-cut Gola 'Barry John' boots. I thought I was the 'bees knees' and, when I proudly paraded them in front of my friends, they very nearly did come up to my knees. Nevertheless, I knew that Barry John was a good player and I thought the boots would make me play like him.

With my Barry John's on, it was totally out of the question that I could even attempt to do any kicking, especially with a big leather rugby ball. Anyway, Quinny took all the penalties and conversions. He was the only one of us with legs big enough to hoist the ball out of the mud.

I remember that around about this time the Welsh were having their 'hay day' and I saw one or two of their games on the telly. The main thing that was going through my mind as I watched the ball travelling up and down the pitch was "Is this the same game ?". It bore no resemblance to the way we played at school. I think it was this lack of understanding of the proper way to play rugby that provided the major contribution towards my decision to accept the milk round.

During the summer term at the Academy we had the choice of cricket or athletics. To be honest, I found cricket rather boring so I tended to concentrate on athletics. To my surprise I found that I was quite good at sprinting, at least in the first year. Over the next few years I was to gradually find my self slipping behind as my friends got bigger. I was obviously a late developer and while everybody else put on muscle and got faster I stayed the same. It wasn't until the late fifth-year or early sixth-year that I was to finally catch them up.

While I was still relatively fast, I managed to win the Victor Ludorum trophy for the most points at the schools sports day. Having won the 200m, the 400m and the 100m hurdles, it put me on level points with Quinny who had won the 100m, the shot-putt and the discus. The teachers decided that I should get the trophy because they reckoned field events didn't really count. I think Quinny is still sore about that one.

I also discovered that I was quite good at cross country, even though I found it tiring. In the second year, not long after the milk round incident, I was entered into the school cross-country team for our age group in the local district championships. Near the end of the race I was about to finish in eleventh position out of around ninety, and I was quite pleased with myself. However my feeling of self-satisfaction was shattered when I saw Mark Livett, one of my friends, crossing the finishing line ahead of me in fourth position. He was more than 200 metres ahead of me which was a total surprise. After the race I went up to him.

"Bloody hell Mark, how did you get up there," I said.

"Oh, I got fed-up and thought I'd take a short-cut," he confessed.

All the rest of the boys in the team finished and we didn't do too badly. However, we were still left with the problem of Mark and the fact that he had been given a tag saying that he had finished fourth. We were worried what Bob Bacon would say, or any of the other boys in our year, if they found out. After a bit of thought we decided that we knew what time Mark should have done and what relative positions we should have finished in. Therefore, we re-arranged our finishing order, giving me the fourth position.

Next day in school assembly it was mentioned that the team had come third and that I had come fourth overall. We all smirked at one another and thought it would be the end of the matter. Unfortunately several days later I found out that the first five home in the race had been chosen to represent London against other top counties. A big thing was made of this in assembly and Bob Bacon was, of course, over the moon. The ironic thing was that he let me off rugby training so I could prepare for the big race.

I was too scared to confess and I trucked off to the race at Epping Forest in North London. It was a freezing cold, wet, windy day and the course had every size of hill in it. During the run I found myself slipping and sliding all over the place wasting a lot of energy. Everybody seemed to pass me with the greatest of ease as if they were running on top of the mud and not in it. Half-way round I started to hate every minute. Nevertheless, I struggled round and came seventy-fourth out of seventy-five runners.

Back on the rugby field, there weren't any large tournaments for us to enter until the fourth year apart from a few sevens trophies. We used to do quite well in the sevens, either winning or coming runners-up, but that was probably down to Quinny more than anything else.

Then, in the fourth year, we were allowed to enter the Medway Cup for all the school teams in Kent. We got through the first rounds, and then we played a school called Howard from Gillingham in the semi-final. The previous time we'd played them we had lost 30-0. (That was on the same day I was running for London; no reflection on me, I think Quinny was ill). This time around we beat them 25-18. Everybody in the team was really ecstatic because it had been our first really big test of ability against a team which usually beat us. The game also sticks in my memory because I scored my first ever drop goal.

By this stage of my life I was beginning to enjoy my rugby because of the camaraderie that was developing in the team. At that sort of age everybody wants to belong to something like a group or a gang, and the rugby team was mine. I didn't think that I was particularly brilliant, but I knew I was good enough to get in to the team and that I contributed to proceedings on the field.

My fifth-year at school (1979/80) started badly and just got worse. I couldn't get into the school first XV rugby team, because I was too small, and I ended up as reserve stand-off for the second team.

School work wasn't to give me much joy either. My mock 'O'-level exams had gone very well and it looked as if I was going to pass most of them fairly easily. However, at the end of the year I was to find out that the real exams were a bit harder. Even so, I was shocked to find out that I had only passed two, English Literature and Art, and failed the rest.

I had quite simply not worked hard enough because I thought I could sit on the laurels of my mock exams. Mum and Dad had encouraged me to study a bit more intensively. But, as an adolescent, I was at the stage of taking any advice as a personal affront and deliberately doing the opposite.

Mum and Dad were upset, I was upset and the teachers were none too happy either. Several options were left open to me. One of them was to re-sit those 'O'-levels which I had failed in the lower-sixth form and stay on for another two years if I wanted to do any 'A'-levels. That's the option which I decided to take.

During the summer, I managed to get a job at a local Irish pub in Lewisham. In that period I managed to put on a couple of stone and grow three inches, thanks mostly to the landlady's cooking and some good stout. The extra weight and height helped my rugby and at the start of the lower-sixth year I was picked for the first XV at fly half. One of the upper-sixth year players, called Tony O'Malley, was playing at full-back and he did all the goal kicking.

My favourite tournament of the year was the floodlit competition run by Askeans Rugby Club. I liked it because it was unusual to play under floodlights, and the games used to attract crowds of around five-hundred compared to our usual thirty. We passed the first round with a victory over St Mary's school from Sidcup and then we came up against Sevenoaks public school in the semi-final.

Although we had a good team with a couple of Kent players, Sevenoaks had the Kent selector as coach, four national-team schoolboys, several county representatives and hadn't been beaten all season. In addition they had just returned from a World Tour, whereas the furthest we had ever been to was Bristol. Naturally, we thought that we were on a 'hiding to nothing' and we would have our hands full just keeping their score in double figures. However, we took the game to them and, on a freezing cold night in mud and rain, we beat them 11-0.

Even though we went on to lose the final against Aske's school from Brockley, Bob Bacon and all us lads were full of pride because of the win over Sevenoaks. We had proven to ourselves and to other schools that we could live with the best.

During the same year I got involved with coaching the first-year and second-year school rugby teams along with a couple of other lads. I found it very enjoyable, especially the teaching aspect, and I decided that I wanted to become a Physical Education teacher. At the end of the year I managed to add four more 'O'-levels to my name - Maths, English Language, Biology and Religious Studies - bringing the total to six. This enabled me to stay at St Joseph's and study for my 'A'-levels which I hoped would get me in to teacher training college. The subjects I chose were English and Biology.

In the upper-sixth year, my first 'A'-level year, we had another very good rugby side. We came up against Sevenoaks again in the semi-final of the floodlight trophy and clocked up another win by 13-6. They also gave us a fixture to play them during the year. It was a great boost to the team and to the school to be awarded such a prestigious game. To everybody's amazement we managed another victory, this time by 12-3, and spirits were very high.

However, the euphoria didn't last very long. A couple of weeks after our third victory over Sevenoaks, Bob Bacon received a 'phone call from them to say that they were dropping St Joseph's from their fixture list. They had found another public school to fill our place.

It didn't make sense for them to drop us at that time because we had beaten them in three matches and, if anything, we were giving them good experience which would have helped to develop a stronger side. Instead we had been dropped because we were a comprehensive school and we didn't fit into their public school set. Irrespective of our rugby playing abilities, we had lost the fixture because our 'faces' didn't fit.

The whole affair served to 'turn-off' our coach and most of the players including myself. It is not surprising that most of the players decided afterwards to stick to football where they weren't exposed to such hassles.

Unfortunately that 'who you know' attitude was prevalent in English Rugby Union at the time. Our school was one of the best sides in Kent, yet at the county trials we managed to get only one player into the Kent side. Perhaps the individual players weren't good enough for the team but if you look at all the school results from the area during the season, you would realise that the selections were crazy. It was the schools with their teachers on the selection panel who had the most players picked for representation.

Apart from that Sevenoaks incident, I was having quite a good time in and out of school. I was made deputy head-boy and Chairman of the school social committee. I also passed my first-year 'A'-level exams and I started playing rugby for London Irish and Askeans.

The Chairmanship of the social committee was thrust upon me rather than by me seeking it. The committee decided that we should arrange a fancy dress party for our all-boys school with local girl's schools, St Theresa's and St Ursula's. No-one volunteered to make the necessary arrangements so I said that I would do the first one but ended up organising them all. Each party went well because we made it blatantly clear to the girls they were not allowed to bring along their boyfriends. We weren't supposed to make any profit and any surplus cash was meant to go to charity, but quite often we each managed to pocket a couple of quid on the side.

At several of the parties I became aware of a girl who I fancied a fair bit. She was head-girl at St Ursula's Catholic convent school and was called Anita. One evening, around about Christmas time, I was out with a few mates in a pub when she walked in with a few of her friends. We got talking and at that point I decided to ask her out.

Egged on by Quinny, I went into W.H.Smith's were Anita worked, picked up some wrapping paper, even though I had half a ton of it back home, and walked over to the long queue in front of her cash desk. There were hundreds of people and it took me nearly twenty minutes even to get near the till. When my turn to be served came around Anita got all embarrassed and ran off, leaving another girl to serve and leaving me to buy some wrapping paper which I didn't need.

Quinny knew Anita a bit better than me and reckoned that I should try again. He said that he had spoken to her and she did actually want to go out with me. This time I decided that I would give her a telephone call, because I thought rejection at the end of a receiver would be less painful than in the flesh. Full of new resolve, I called her up and, being a master of smart chat-up lines, said, "Do you want to go out with me ?". She said, "Yes" and that was that. For our first date, I continued to show my suave sophistication with women, and took her down to the local pub where we sat and talked.

I had been hoping to impress Anita by getting my driving licence, but my hopes were a little misplaced. When the day of my test came around, Dad took me for a final lesson to practice reversing which I hadn't done before. On the first attempt I backed around a corner near the local hospital and promptly flattened a young tree. Policeman Dad just said to slap the car into forward gear and to get out of there, which I did.

After that little warm-up, Dad drove me down to the test centre at Hither Green. I set off with the instructor in our old 'L'-registration maroon Ford Cortina after the basic eye tests and, at the first junction, put on the left indicator. As it had done many times before, it became stuck. The instructor told me to pull over to the side and to stop the car. He then got out and went around the back to see if the light was working. While he was walking round I started flicking the indicator handle up and down to make it flash. Unfortunately he saw me through the back window and failed me on the spot, just half a mile from the test centre.

Kieran found out that I had failed and called up to console me which I thought was nice of him. Not so. The next day, I was walking down to Blackheath from school at lunch time and his car passed me. Kieran was driving and a load of my other 'friends' were hanging out of the windows. All the car lights were on, the windscreen wipers were going, the horn was blaring and they threw me a set of 'L'-plates. For the whole of the next week, I was the subject of one long mickey-take.

My final year at St Joseph's (1982/83) started well but ended badly. I passed both my mock 'A'-levels and, having gained another couple of inches, I moved out to centre in the rugby team. I was also made the team captain. We got through to the final of the floodlit competition for the third time but we lost again, this time 0-3 to Chislehurst and Sidcup, a team whom we had beaten by about twenty points the year before.

I still wanted to be a P.E. teacher and I applied to go to St Mary's college in London to study for a Bachelor of Arts in Human Movement and to Cardiff College to study for a Bachelor of Education. Both colleges provisionally accepted me with a requirement of just two passes at 'A'-level.

School-work had slid down in my list of priorities, behind rugby and socialising. As a result I repeated my trick of sitting on the laurels of my mock exam results, not really putting much effort into studying. Even though the exams seemed difficult I thought that I'd scraped the passes which I required.

The day the results came out was a hot summer's day in August. I knew that they were due so I walked down the road to meet the postman and persuaded him to hand over the letter. I took it over to the park, and sat on a grassy bank looking at it for several minutes before I plucked up courage to open it.

To tell you the truth I couldn't believe it, even though in my heart-of-hearts I knew what it was going to say. I had failed both of them. They weren't even grade O's, which meant "just failed", but grade F's for "go away".

I sat there staring into space with that numb feeling as if the world had just dropped away from beneath me. What was I going to do now ? If I'd been able to go to college then I would have been effectively looked after for a few more years but now I was on my own. I realised that it was all my own stupid fault for not putting in enough work and anger towards myself crept into my emotions.

After nearly an hour, and a few frustrated tears, I picked myself up and went to tell my parents. They, too, were devastated but came out with those kind words of encouragement which parents do. I can't remember exactly what they suggested I should do because my mind was in so much of a spin.

That evening I went out for a few beers with my mates in the pub to drown my sorrows. During the evening, an inspiration just came to me - I would join the police force with Dad. When I got home, I announced my plans. Dad was happy but Mum wasn't so keen on the idea having been married to a policeman for many years. The biggest surprise to my announcement, however, came from Mike. He had decided that he wasn't going anywhere with his job as a technician so he said that he was going to apply with me !

Dad got us the forms which we sent off, and we were both invited to Victoria police station for some initial interviews and a physical check-up. The physical was fairly easy, and the interview wasn't too tough either, just a bit harder than the one I'd been given when starting at St Joseph's. We were both told we'd passed the first stage interviews and were invited to attend the second stage, but on different days.

I went first and found it a bit more difficult. This time the interviews lasted a full day, and at the end I was made to wait in a queue with everybody else to find out the final result of my application. I thought that having a father in the Metropolitan police would be in my favour. However, fears started to grow when the lad in front of me, who had just dropped out of a law degree at university, was told that he hadn't got in. After five minutes of worry, I was called into the main office. From the look on the faces of everybody in there, I thought I was going to be rejected as well. But fortunately I was wrong and they dourly informed me that I'd got in. One or two weeks later, Mike went along and was told that his application had also been successful. We were both delighted, and called up to find out that our training was scheduled to start at Hendon Police College in March 1984.

Although failing my 'A'-levels was to prove a bigger influence on my life, the Sevenoaks farce had upset me just as much. In my opinion, the schools situation was a reflection on the state of senior Rugby Union at the time. If you were not part of the establishment then you could not hope to have an equal say in things. Unfortunately, to be accepted meant having money.

The whole system needed a good shake up because the 'upper class' public-school types had ruled the game for too long. They didn't need money to play the game and they wanted to keep outside influences to a minimum so they could have it for themselves. It was reminiscent of those days back in 1895 when the Northern Unions decided to split and to allow broken-time payments. Players with skill were still being driven out of the game if they didn't 'fit'. The same went for decent coaches, if they didn't toe the line of the ruling bodies they were hassled out of the game at an early age.

Thankfully, in the last ten years, the British system seems to have started sorting itself out. The move towards a divisional based structure and the recent decisions to allow players to capitalise (in some ways) on their talent is a step in the right direction. However, I believe that they will need to go further down that route if they are to generate quality teams consistently.

The 'system' in New Zealand allows everybody to get a fair chance, irrespective of background, race, colour or creed. It has worked so well because the cream of the players have been allowed to rise to the top. There hasn't been any single group of people, like the public schools, trying to protect themselves and ignoring all those who were not in 'their' circles.

These days people often ask me if I think I would have made it into the English or Irish teams if I had stayed in London rather than going to New Zealand. The answer is a definite No ! I would probably just be a spectator at Highbury, watching Arsenal each week.

Chapter 3

Right Time, Right Place

At the end of 1982, when I was eighteen and still at school, I started training with London Irish at Sunbury in south-west London. It was a long way to travel from Lewisham but I found the extra coaching very helpful. When a chance came up to go on tour with the under-twenty-one side to Dublin at Easter in 1983, I took it. The side had two games arranged, both as curtain raisers for the first team, on Good Friday and Easter Sunday. The first match was against Bective Rangers on a very muddy pitch. Not many of us could stand up for long, let alone play rugby, and we lost the game. The first team, on the other hand, were a bit more adept in the poor conditions and they snatched a narrow win.

On Saturday everybody went to watch Ireland versus England at Lansdowne Road. Ollie Campbell scored a try and kicked several goals in a strong wind to give Ireland a rousing victory over England by 25-15. That evening I was invited over to the plush Shelbourne Hotel where the teams were staying. I remember being introduced to Ollie and to Dusty Hare, who, of course, didn't know me from a bar of soap and probably still won't remember the meeting. However, it had a large impact on me. Brushing shoulders with and talking to those great players made me yearn to be part of the same 'club'.

The next day we had our second game against a side from Clontarf. It was another tiring game on a sticky ground which pulled at everyone's leg muscles. We lost the game despite scoring four tries because of eight penalty goals against us, and I remember coming off feeling fairly tired. As I plodded into the changing rooms after the game, the first team manager pulled me to one side. He slowly went through a story which, when abbreviated, meant that he didn't know where the first team full-back was. Whether the player was missing in London or in Dublin didn't matter, he wasn't there and I was needed to substitute for him in the first team game.

I consulted my tired legs who begged me to cry-off but I heard myself replying in the positive, "That would be great, when's the game?".

"In about twenty minutes," he replied.

"I won't have time for a shower then," I said because I was filthy.

"That doesn't matter, we'll find you a new shirt and pair of shorts," he smiled.

So, only minutes after finishing the under-twenty-one game, I trotted out with the first team in a clean jersey several sizes too big for me and a pair of baggy shorts.

My fatigue meant that I didn't have a great part to play in the game, but I kept my concentration and made sure that I didn't make any enormous mistakes. The pace was a lot higher than it had been in my first game and it was a very physical confrontation. Luckily the ball didn't get thrown out wide too often so I didn't have to do too much running. Even so, I began to see stars in the last twenty minutes and I could feel my legs starting to buckle beneath me. We won and I wish I could say I enjoyed it but I was too tired.

That evening, and on the ferry back home, all the rest of the players laid into the Guinness. It seemed to be a continuous party and everybody was enjoying themselves. Everybody, that was, except me; I just sat in a corner with a big overcoat on, fast asleep.

A few weeks after my return from Dublin, I received a 'phone call from Askeans saying that they had a few injury problems in their team. They had heard on the grapevine that I'd played for London Irish, so would I come along and sub for them in a local Kent game. Thinking that it was rather nice to be in demand by an established club, I didn't explain that I had only played because the first choice full-back had gone missing. Instead I accepted the invitation as if it were an everyday occurrence.

I managed to beg a lift to the game, got changed and took up my position on a rather rickety old bench next to the team coach. During the first half one of the Askeans wingers got injured in a tackle and had to come off at half-time. The coach nodded in my direction and I was on. Again I concentrated on not making a fool of myself particularly in defence. A fair number of kicks came my way but I either managed to get under them or I had a lucky bounce. The end result was that I had a good game and we won the match. Unfortunately for one of the other players, he didn't have such a good time as me and he got badly injured.

After the game, the coach congratulated me on my play and then explained that the player who had got injured in the second half was one of their sevens players. Since Askeans had just qualified for the Middlesex Sevens, he asked me if I would be free to go along and play for them at Twickenham. What a fantastic break of luck. After only half a game in the Askeans Jersey they wanted me to play for them in one of the top tournaments. The whole thing was just pure good fortune and I didn't want to let it slip by; so, after a short pause, I agreed.

The following week I turned up at Twickenham in plenty of time and listened intently to the advice of the other team members. We had been drawn against Waterloo in the first round and we thought we had a good chance. When the time came for us to play we all wished one another luck and trotted out onto the pitch. There were about fifty thousand in the stands and the noise was stunning. I was totally overawed and, unfortunately, that's the way I stayed all game.

We lost 12-0 and I hardly made any contribution, being in a dream for the whole match. The rest of my day was spent in a gloomy mood sitting in the stands and watching Richmond win the tournament for their ninth time by beating London Welsh 20-13. I knew that it had been my big chance. In front of a huge crowd and with the games being shown on Rugby Special, I'd blown it. Over the next few weeks my confidence took a severe nose-dive. I had wasted my shot at the big time and with the public schools set-up I was hardly likely to get another. The lack of confidence in my own abilities and in the English Rugby Union system, coupled with depression about my 'A'-level results, were to make me virtually give up playing rugby altogether.

I was still very disillusioned with the game of rugby when, in October of 1983, I was invited to a twenty-first birthday party for Pete Livett, Mark's brother. It was just before I applied to the police.

There was a big crowd of people there including Tony O'Malley who had played full-back for St Joseph's first XV when I'd been in fifth-year and he'd been in the upper sixth-year. Tony had not long returned from an exciting trip down to New Zealand. He had been playing rugby for a season at a club called Oriental Rongotai, less formally known as Ories.

Tony had originally been invited to New Zealand by Bernie Parish, one of our ex-teachers from St Joseph's, who had emigrated a few years earlier. Bernie had started coaching the Ories second team to help out someone called Clive Currie who was coaching the first team. When Clive had found himself short of a full-back and a goal kicker in 1982, Bernie had arranged for an English player called Murray Jones from Stourbridge to go over and play. The venture had been successful with Murray scoring more than 100 points for the club. The following season another player was asked out to fill the same position, this had been Tony. He had followed in Murray's footsteps and played very well in the first team. However, Tony had gone one better and been the top points scorer with 189 points in the Wellington club competition during 1983. Ories had asked Tony to return for the following season in 1984. He had reluctantly turned them down saying that he would like to come back but not for the following season, perhaps the one after.

When I heard the story from Tony at the party I had jokingly said, "Put my name down for next year if you don't change your mind", expecting him to laugh it off. However, he said that he had heard that I'd played for London Irish on a tour of Ireland and that I'd played for Askeans in the Middlesex Sevens so he would, indeed, put my name forward. I didn't have the heart or the inclination to tell him the full story and to explain that my escapades sounded grander than they actually were.

Being unsure of what Tony would do and what would come of it, I started playing rugby again for the Askeans' fourth team. I was rusty to start with but it wasn't long before I made it through the ranks of the third and second teams into the first team where I occasionally played as winger or centre.

On my twentieth birthday, 29th January 1984, we had a game near Watford and after the match we went for a quick pint or two. Unfortunately, when we came to get on the dilapidated old coach to go home, we discovered that the driver was blind drunk. By the time he had sobered up, we had got more drunk and I had missed a rendezvous with my friends back in a Lewisham pub. Hoping they'd still be there when I got back, I went to look for them with no luck. Eventually I decided to return to another of my locals where another couple of my friends helped me to celebrate. It was a long night and I finally rolled home at about 3 a.m. the next day.

At 7 a.m. the 'phone rang disturbing me from my slumber and Mum answered. It was Clive Currie calling from New Zealand. She quickly ran upstairs and pulled me out of bed even though I was suffering from a severe hangover. Clive's voice was very faint against the thumping in my head but I could just about make out the words. He said that he was looking for a goal-kicking full-back to go to New Zealand in March and he had heard that I was interested. I simply replied that I was and Clive rang off.

A few weeks later a short letter of confirmation arrived. It was only at this point that I realised I didn't know how to play at full-back and that I didn't kick many goals. Luckily there were still nearly three months to go before they wanted me to fly out, so I spent most of my spare time at the practice ground.

In the meantime, Anita had gone off to St Mary's College for teacher training and we were only seeing one another every three to four weeks. The relationship consequently became a bit strained and, when we talked, we started to realise that it wasn't going anywhere even though we agreed that we still liked one another. At the tender ages of nineteen and twenty neither of us wanted to make any long term commitments. As a result we just drifted further and further apart.

The lack of romantic ties, the backing of my parents and a desire to do something for myself helped me finally to decide that I would go down under. I sent my own scribbled letter of confirmation and started to wet myself with worry.

I also wrote a bit more formally to the police and asked if my entry could be deferred for six months while I went to New Zealand. They replied saying that I could, probably because they like their new entrants to be as mature as possible.

Clive Currie sent me another letter, this time with a few more details of what would be required of me, such as helping with the coaching of the junior teams. Then I got a letter from a Mr D.D.Bond describing himself as the Director of Immigration. The letter said that he would try to get me involved with a family when I was over there, that they would try to find me some sort of a job and that there shouldn't be any problem with immigration ! This only added to my worry, in fact it made me petrified. What had I let myself in for ? I was just an ordinary rugby player who had lied about being able to play full-back and to kick goals. I wasn't even on the verge of being picked for a representative side. I'd been asked out to New Zealand to play rugby on the strength of my good fortune at London Irish and Askeans, and now I had the New Zealand Director of Immigration writing to me. I asked Tony and he helped put me at ease by saying that Don Bond had been connected with the Oriental Rongotai rugby club for most of his adult life and took a deep interest in what went on.

To fill in the time and to earn some cash before I was to due fly out I decided to get a job. Kieran's Dad ran a building company so he persuaded him to let me have a short-term job as a general labourer.

The first site I worked on was at Gatwick Airport. I had to get up at 4:45 a.m. to be at New Cross for 5:30 a.m. where I was picked up with a lot of other Irish navvies in an ancient green transit van. We would then splutter around London calling at several pubs picking up the missing members of the work-crew where they had been left the night before. The van would eventually arrive at the airport around about 7:15 a.m. for work to start at 7:30 a.m. on the dot.

The first thing that I was told to do was to help with the preparation of a ditch to make a culvert. The method involved pouring several thin layers of concrete over some reinforcing braided-steel cables. My job was to go around the cables knocking the spare concrete off with a short hammer before the next layer was poured on.

On the first day, I had been deeply engrossed in this most rewarding of exercises for nearly three long hours when I vaguely heard the toot of a van's horn. I peered over the edge of the ditch to see that the area where there had previously been nearly twenty people eagerly working away was now empty. To the right, I just caught a glimpse of a half-exposed Irish backside disappearing over an embankment, so I quickly jumped out and followed it. Over the bank was the green van with everybody inside it, about to set off. I sprinted down to it and just managed to jump on the back as it took off. I asked what was going on, "Breakfast" was the only answer. We arrived at the canteen nearly a mile away and I was nearly killed in the rush as they all piled out over my head before the van had even stopped. By the time I found my way up to the canteen and got served with my plate of grease, they were all sat around with empty plates, fags in their mouths and all reading tabloid newspapers. Five minutes later they had all disappeared again and I had to race back outside to catch the van back to the site.

Every day we used to finish work at about 5:30 p.m. and then drive back in to London. The trip would only take about an hour but the Irish boys always decided that they wanted a drink on the way. I wouldn't get back home until about 9 p.m. and, because I had to get up so early, I spent most of that Gatwick job as a zombie, hardly able to keep my eyes open. I would have said something to them about the drinking but I was a fresh faced twenty year-old. They, on the other hand, were all a lot older, had been everywhere, done everything and got all the T-shirts, so, if they wanted to drink, who was I to argue. It was all 'learn as you go' stuff and nobody ever told me what to do but I suppose it was my introduction to 'real life'.

Chapter 4

A Flying Start

Mum, Dad and Pat took me to the airport in the car. I could tell that Mum was a bit upset at the thought of my departure. She shed a few tears but not too many because she knew it wasn't going to be for long and that I'd be back in a short six months.

I was on a British Airways flight and I found myself seated near the back of the rather cramped economy class, sandwiched between two huge men. The air was filled with an overpowering odour, not too dissimilar to the after-effects of a final fling in the curry house. Both of them were so big that I couldn't put my arms on the arm-rest and I had to spend the entire first part of the journey with my elbows digging in to their flabby hips.

We stopped in Muscat to refuel but there was a strike going on amongst some of the airport staff which meant that we couldn't get off the plane to stretch our legs. To make matters worse, the air conditioning inside the plane wasn't working. As the temperature rose in the cabin everyone began to get very hot and my travelling companions started sweating profusely. One of the air-stewardesses thought that she would help to cool the cabin by opening a door which was a bad move because the outside air temperature was even higher. Next stop was Bombay and I remember looking out of the window to see the local lads playing football on some grass next to the runway. They cleared off as the plane landed and then re-appeared afterwards to continue with their game. Both of my 'close' companions got off and the air conditioning was fixed.

That left me with just one discomfort remaining - my own thoughts - and they managed to keep me awake for the rest of the journey. I was worried that I wouldn't live up to the expectations of the people who had invited me out to New Zealand. Such a failure would leave me down there with no friends and no family but I would still have to stay for the full six months. On the plus side, I knew that I was getting the chance to 'start again' after my exam failures and that was a marvellous opportunity which was unlikely to repeat itself.

My worrying seemed to make time pass quickly and before long we had landed in Auckland. I cleared customs with no problems and caught an internal flight to Wellington. As I walked in to the arrivals lounge, I was met by three men. I recognised the guy in the middle as Clive Currie from pictures that I had seen of him when he was playing for the All Blacks. The other two were around about the same age, same height but neither of them could be called slim. One of them was wearing a smart collar and tie with a neat short-back-and-sides haircut and looked fairly official. The other also had a tie on but he had ruffled hair and half a cigarette hanging out of the side of his mouth.

I spoke first, saying "Hello" to Clive. He shook my hand and asked me about the flight. Then he turned to introduce me to the others. Stepping in ahead of him, I looked towards the man in the suit and said, "You must be Mr Bond, the Director of Immigration !". "No," was the reply, "I'm Dave Thurlow, the secretary of Oriental Rongotai. You'll be staying with my family and me during the first few months of your stay". I apologised and turned to Mr Bond. He flicked back his hair so that he could see me and said "Hi", then added that I should call him Don, not Mr Bond. I looked at him in amazement: this was the Director of Immigration for New Zealand and he wasn't wearing a dull pin-stripe suit. It made me realise, right there and then, that Wellington was going to be a very different place to London and I started to relax straight away. These were just ordinary people and I was going to be OK.

Don and Clive went on ahead leaving Dave and I to pack my bags into his car for the short drive to his home. The Thurlow's house was in a suburb of Wellington called Miramar, only a couple of miles from the airport. The garage was next to the roadside but you had to go down about thirty evenly placed concrete steps to get to the front door. The house itself was a low-built wooden-construction residence, more like a bungalow, with a nice view right across Miramar.

Dave and his wife, Maureen, lived there with their son and daughter called Brian and Sue, who were about my age. They also had an older son called Ross who was living and working in Australia at the time. Dave worked in the police, while his wife worked in a pharmacy. I remember thinking that it was going to be great having a ready-made family to look after me. After a delicious roast dinner and the usual 'first meeting' chat, I retired to bed so I could sleep off my journey and replace the nervous energy that I'd expended. I was sharing a bedroom with Brian but I didn't even hear him come in.

Clive gave me a couple of days to acclimatise and then came round to pick me up in his car. He took me back to meet his wife, Jill, and then he gave me a bit of a run-down on the history of Oriental Rongotai or 'Ories' as they were known.

Ories played in the Wellington area's First Division. The standard of the division was reasonably high but not 'top-flight' (roughly on a level with the lower sections of the English third division which was to come into existence). The fourteen teams in the first division played one another once in what was called the Swindale Shield series, with the winning team taking the Shield. The top eight clubs would then play-off for the Jubilee Cup whilst the bottom six were joined by the top two teams of the second division to play-off for the Hardham Cup. The bottom two teams of the Hardham Cup would then be relegated to the second division. Ories had always finished near the bottom of the first division or the top of the second division. However, the previous year, 1983, with the help of Tony O'Malley, they had won the Hardham Cup. Clive's target for 1984 was to finish in the top eight and join the play-offs for the Jubilee Cup.

The club's rugby ground was owned by the council which meant that it was closed until the start of the playing season. Therefore, training used to take place at the nearby Rongotai College secondary school. My first training session was three days after I'd arrived and I knew it was going to be a 'big' one. Tony had implanted in my brain that New Zealand rugby players love a 'trier'. He had seen me play once or twice and said I would probably be the quickest in the team. He also reckoned the skill level would be much the same as I had been used to in London. The main difference, he said, was going to be in the level of fitness and the playing attitude. I had to impress from day one despite some lingering jet-lag. I knew it was going to be difficult and to add to the problem it was 'pre-season training' which is always harder than regular training.

I was introduced to the team one by one and I was immediately struck by the number of different face shapes. There was Maori, Western Samoan, Tongan, Raratongan and Pakeha (the white man).

Even the Pakeha were tanned and my lily white skin stood out a mile. After a lot of in-depth thought and intellectual discussion amongst the team they gave me the nickname of 'Pommie'.

One of the things that helped my integration with the regular Ories players was the fact that I wasn't 'taking' one of their places. They had become used to the idea of there being an 'import' in the team with Murray Jones and Tony O'Malley. Since both Murray and Tony had done well, the players didn't mind too much. Of course, this indirectly put more pressure on me to live up to their higher-than-normal expectations.

That first training session started with a long run, then some 400m sprints working down to 50m and all interspersed with some ball skills. The session lasted about two and a half hours and, conscious of what Tony had said, I tried to win every single sprint while doing my best in the drills. At the end of the session I was totally and utterly drained. My tongue was stuck to the roof of my mouth, my lips were dry and my face was caked in salt. On the way out I'd seen a newly fitted metal water tap on a wall adjacent to the changing rooms so I slowly jogged over for a drink. As I got there one of the props called Steve Cox also reached for the same tap. Steve was thick-set and looked to me like a Maori but he was, in fact, of Slavic descent. He took one look at me, decided that my need was greater and waved me on to drink first.

Coxy was also fresh at the club that year and was about the same age as me but he was much more worldly-wise. He had left school at sixteen and had played a few games for Ories. At the age of nineteen he had gone over to Australia and found work on a fleet fishing boat for three months. After about ten days at sea he had learnt that he didn't have any sea-legs because he was throwing-up all the time. He had been saved from another two-and-a-half months of seasickness when he developed an abscess on his tooth. Not being able to do his work properly he was dropped off on an a small island in Malaysia to have it fixed. When his time was up, Clive had offered him a place back at Ories and he grabbed it with both arms. Because Coxy was one of the few single guys at the club and he had no family in the area, much the same as me, we became really good friends.

Apart from Coxy, the majority of my friends in those early days were married, which was great for me as a bachelor. All of them regularly asked me round to their houses for meals and I would be able to decide where I wanted to go each night. It was really kind of them because they knew that I would never be able to return the compliment. I think they all thought that I was completely useless at looking after myself, like a fish out of water, and they were right.

We would describe him as being well-mannered, polite, fun-loving and a totally likeable young man. If he had any shortcomings it would have been his great liking for food and his untidiness in the bedroom.

One amusing incident I can recall did centre around food. He had spent his afternoon at Hutt Valley and on his way home to Miramar felt hungry so called at McDonald's. He demolished two Big Macs and chips. He then came home and at about 5:30pm sat down to a full roast dinner followed by dessert. All of which was disposed of with his usual relish. We had just finished dining when the telephone rang. I answered it, and when John heard who I was speaking to, he leapt up, grabbed the handpiece and told the caller that he had not forgotten and that he was just leaving. He had been invited out to dinner and had forgotten. However, without revealing all he kept the appointment and ended up having a second roast dinner and dessert.

DAVE THURLOW

My first match for Ories was on the 11th March. It was a friendly against a team called Red Star from Masterton in Wairarapa Bush. It was about an hour and a half away by coach and I hate coach journeys at the best of times. In between the Wellington province and The Wairarapa province there is a big hill or, more accurately, a mini mountain range called the Rimutaka. Each side has very steep and extremely windy roads which made me feel really sick.

By the time we arrived at Red Star and went out onto the field I was a fainter shade of green. My colour went well with the Ories kit which I put on for the first time; black and white hoops with yellow cuffs and collar, black shorts and black and white hooped socks.

Not long after the start we got a scrum on the half-way line. The ball came out of the base of the scrum to Mark Bracewell. He missed out John Gloag and passed to Tom Vitale at centre. Having recovered a little, I ran up outside of Tom, screaming for the ball. He gave me a perfect pass, allowing me to cut inside the full-back and cover to score under the posts - a try with my first touch of the ball ! Having scored under the sticks, I was also left with an easy conversion for my first kick.

About ten minutes later Red Star were on attack when they dropped the ball. I managed to get to it first, and then kicked it all the way up the field, soccer-style, to score again. A second try with my second touch of the ball - what a dream start. The final score was 18-9 in our favour with me scoring 14 points. I was greatly relieved because I'd managed to lift some of the pressure off my shoulders. To add to my joy, Don Bond was watching from the side, still with his hair in his eyes and a cigarette hanging from the side of his mouth.

Off the rugby field, I was introduced by Don to Colin Nelson Harrington Bridge, or Bridgey for short. Bridgey looked a bit like the botanist David Bellamy with a big frame and a bushy beard. He had been the Ories coach a few years before Clive. In Wellington, he ran a crib-walling business (a crib wall is a reinforcing wall which is put up against a bank or existing wall to stop it collapsing) and helped out by giving me a job. We used to pick up the crib walls from a concrete block manufacturers or concrete-pie factory as we called it, where Coxy worked. We would then take them down to the site, which needed re-enforcing, in a beaten-up old truck.

My first day at work was a really hot day. Bridgey had said that he would pick me up at 7:30 a.m. but this came and went with no sign of him. Three quarters of an hour later he called the house to say that he had overslept and that he would be over in twenty minutes. At 9 a.m. he finally arrived and we went down to the concrete-pie factory. Successfully loaded, we drove at a leisurely speed down to the site at Berhampore. This work-site itself was next to Athletic Park where the Wellington provincial side play. The bank which needed reinforcing was above another bank, which meant that we had to carry the crib-blocks up about seventy-five steps to lay them. Bridgey looked at the bank, then at me and rolled his eyes.

The people who owned the site were friends of Bridgey and that's how he had got the work. We went up and knocked at the door to announce our arrival. The lady of the house asked us in for a cup of tea and a slice of cake before she went to work. We had a bit of a chat afterwards and this took about half an hour.

Eventually Bridgey indicated that we better get started, so we went down to the top bank and started digging a ditch for the base of the crimps. After about another half hour, he put down his spade and said that it was 'Smoko' time, the New Zealand equivalent of a British 'Tea Break'. We went back to the house, where the lady had left some food in the kitchen. After another cup of tea and cake we sat and talked about rugby for about an hour. Bridgey had played some representative rugby for Otago on the south island and also played for Ories before he turned to coaching. This brought the time up to about 11 a.m. so we went to do some more work.

There were about two-hundred of the concrete crimp-blocks to carry up the steps of the lower bank. After an hour of this strenuous work, Bridgey announced that it was lunchtime. Lunch took about an hour and a half because Bridgey just loved his rugby and wouldn't stop talking about it. We returned to work in the heat. This time we lasted three-quarters of an hour before he turned round and looked at me.

"Have you had enough, Pommie ?" he asked.

"Well it's up to you," I replied.

"Yeh, I've had enough. Let's go down the bar," and he walked off to the truck. I followed and we went down to his favourite drinking hole. Several beers were drunk while discussing the inevitable rugby and how hard my first day at work had been. It wasn't until about 10 p.m. that I got back home.

The rest of my time with Bridgey wasn't quite so leisurely. However, when he did his estimates for work he continued to add on a couple of days for Smoko-time and for chats.

After a couple of months with Bridgey a new job was offered to me by the Wellington Rugby Union. The job entailed going round all the schools in the area coaching rugby and naturally I took it. One of the side benefits was that it gave me some mobility, because the Swindale Shield sponsors provided me with a nice new stationwagon. The Union also helped me out with my expenses.

I would ring round the schools on a Friday afternoon and arrange to visit them the following week. It was hard work to start with but, as my rugby season went on, I became better known in the area and used to be greeted with some sort of recognition, rather than just as a Pommie teaching rugby.

My plan was to spend about an hour at each school. Most of the kids were running around in bare feet and they were all really keen. But, it didn't take long for me to realise that they just wanted to run around and have a laugh. Correspondingly I cut back my coaching to forty minutes and then started to throw a ball into their midst for them to have a quick 'game' . It reminded me of Wednesdays at St Joseph's secondary school. Usually they would start playing roughly but, when threatened with another ten minutes of drills if the play got out of hand, they always calmed down. My aim was for all of the kids to go home and say that they had been playing rugby and that they had enjoyed themselves. If they went home and said that they had played rugby but it was boring because of all the drills, then the object would have been lost.

I was to continue working for the Union, mostly coaching with short spells in their office, until the end of my first stay in New Zealand. I thoroughly enjoyed my time and it made me wish even more that I had passed my exams to enable me to go on and be a Physical Education instructor. But then, if I had, I wouldn't have got the break to go to New Zealand and I might have given up playing rugby altogether.

My performance in the friendly against Red Star helped to get me a place in the first XV for Ories opening league game of the season at Porirua. Clive used to name the team on a Thursday night before training, and when he told me I'd got a place for the game I started to relax a bit more. At least I was being given the chance to prove myself rather than having to wait for someone to get injured.

After they heard that I'd been picked, everybody congratulated me then told me that the league would be totally different to friendlies. This started to make me worry again; was I going to be able to stand the pace ? I confided in Bridgey and he took me to see the Wellington Centurions against the Auckland Barbarians to help take my mind off Ories' game.

The participating teams basically consisted of the best players from both provinces with a few 'ringers' thrown in, and the game was essentially an All Black trial. Looking through the programme I recognised names such as Andy Haden, Stu Wilson and Murray Mexted. Although it was probably important in terms of selection, it was also a 'fun' game. The ball was thrown about the pitch at very high speed and there was a lot of open play. I was mesmerised. There was also one young player who not many people had heard of until that game when he scored three tries, John Kirwan. I was full of admiration for the way he played and was surprised to find out that he was a year younger than me.

After the game, Bridgey took me to the Wellington Hotel where the players were staying.

"Come on, let's go in for a drink," He said.

"Don't be daft," I replied, "we can't go in there".

"It'll be alright," he answered and disappeared off somewhere. A few minutes later he was back with some tickets to go in. Apparently his brother Geoff was 'high-up' in the Wellington executive.

Once inside we got a drink and Bridgey went to see one of the players he knew well. While he was away I just stood alone in bewilderment. John Kirwan was nearby and I could tell he was a couple of inches taller than me but otherwise we were fairly similar. That made me think that maybe I wouldn't be as good as him but I could certainly do alright; maybe one day...

Bridgey returned and we carried on talking. I definitely wasn't going to reveal my thoughts to him in case he reckoned that I was getting big-headed. We drank up and left. As we were going out I had this sense that I wanted to be part of that 'scene' inside, with all the top players. But I still had it all to do and the hard work was about to begin the next day.

It was a fairly warm day at Porirua Park with the wind coming down from the North. We won the toss and conceded the wind for the first half. Right from kick-off the game was played at a high pace which suited our pack who were very fit and highly mobile. As a result we dominated most phases of the game. The pressure was very definitely being put on the home side and very soon they gave us a penalty. It wasn't going to be an easy kick but neither did it look difficult. I took my run-up and sliced it to the right, missing the posts by quite a bit. I turned and ran back with my head down. Missing a penalty was no big thing but this was going to be an important game for me and it hadn't started too well.

After 22 minutes we got another penalty in nearly the same spot. Words of encouragement were shouted at me from our pack as I placed the ball. This time it sailed between the posts and we were in the lead. Some good touch kicking kept us in Porirua's territory for most of the first half. Mark Bracewell took full advantage 10 minutes after my penalty when he landed a great drop goal. At half-time we went in leading 0-6.

In the second half we had the wind in our favour. This, combined with our better fitness, meant that we remained well in command of the game. I kicked another couple of penalties and then Wayne de Terte intercepted a Porirua pass to start a fifty metre move which he finished with a try. Soon after, I came outside Dominic Barnao on the right wing. He wasn't too fast because he was more of a stand-off rather than a winger, so he passed the ball out to me. I was tackled as I was about to cross the try line but managed to place the ball in the corner to score what I thought was my first competition try. I got up and was as pleased as punch. Then I noticed the referee was signalling that I hadn't grounded the ball.

The decision had annoyed me but I didn't let it get me down. About five minutes later, there was an identical situation with me touching the ball down just as I was being tackled. Fortunately this time the referee awarded the try. I then managed to land the conversion from the touchline to add to my joy. Another penalty a few minutes later gave us a 0-22 lead which we held on for the last 20 minutes. When the final whistle blew I was ecstatic. Not only had we won our first game by a large margin but I had scored 15 of the points.

That first win cheered everybody in the team and gave us two points in the league. This was when I noticed a difference between rugby in New Zealand and rugby in England. Every time Ories went out, there were two league points at stake. None of the games were played 'just for a laugh'. Each match was therefore played with a greater intensity which led to players having to improve their game to stay in a good team.

With there being so much pressure placed on all the players in every game this naturally led to a good national side in New Zealand. Emerging international players who were just getting into the All Blacks for the first time didn't have to get used to the importance of winning as well as to a new playing style. And history shows that this attitude must have been right. Whilst the All Blacks may not have always been the best team in the world, they have always been up there or thereabouts.

The recent introduction of a similar system in Britain should help to strengthen the national sides. However results shouldn't be judged in just one or two seasons even if one side, such as England, go well for a while. Success should only be proclaimed when the same side stays at the top for a number of years, say at least five.

Clive was particulary happy with my performance against Porirua which was great because it meant that he gave me a bit more attention in training. On top of that he used to take me aside afterwards and give me lots of little tips about where to stand and what to do. In essence, he taught me the correct way to play the full-back position.

Every Friday he would pick me up in town when he had finished teaching at a local school in Wellington. We would then go up to the park with a couple of match balls and I would practice kicking for about an hour. If I missed three kicks in a row he would come over and make me change my action ever so slightly. If it worked, then he would try to make it better. If it didn't, then he would make me start again. It was his repetitive attention to detail that made me a better player all round. Clive made me concentrate more and think about the different facets of my game, rather than just going out on the field to start playing.

The fact that I managed to get a bit more attention in training was just because I was a new boy. Normally Clive was totally dedicated to making all of his team into better players. We also had a Samoan half-back called Sale Tevita. I remember Clive taking him to the side one day and start throwing a ball against the changing room wall for Sale to catch and to pass to one side or the other. For more than an hour he kept Sale there, catching the ball and passing it to either side normally or as a spin pass off the ground.

My first impressions of John were that he was a pale, gangly and somewhat awkward player. However, these impressions quickly disappeared during the first games of the season as his raw natural ability, exceptional pace and flair for rugby became evident.

He showed particular qualities which were to earmark him for the top; an ability to change pace and swerve past opponents; a capacity to turn defensive situations into attack; perfect timing when hitting the back line; a strong positional sense; the ability to shut down attackers with the ball in hand; and a capability to take the high ball under pressure.

He was also raw in more than one respect. My wife, Jill, and I had John round for a meal shortly after his arrival. Having enjoyed a number of dishes of Chinese food it was time for dessert. John was informed that in New Zealand it was customary to eat ice cream with chopsticks. Being the polite guest, and without so much as a doubting look, he proceeded to devour the plate of ice cream using his chopsticks.
CLIVE CURRIE

Our second game was on the Wednesday evening, our first under floodlights, at our own Hutt Recreation Ground. The visiting opposition were Wellington College Old Boys who had beaten Ories the year before and finished fourth in the league. Being systematic, Clive had made a schedule for us to finish in the top eight of the Swindale Shield. Each game was marked as to whether he thought we could win it or not. Those games which he didn't envisage we would win and which we didn't need in order to finish in the top eight were marked as 'bonus' games. Obviously he didn't tell us but he had the WCOB match down as one of his bonus games.

It was a very tough game but we played to our well-rehearsed game plan and seemed to be holding our own. However a certain amount of luck seemed to be going the way of WCOB and they had a couple of rather dodgy penalties about mid-way through the first half to make it 0-6 against us. We thought that this was going to be the score at the break but unfortunately a defensive error just before the whistle let them score a rather fortuitous try and we trailed in 0-10.

Clive gave us a rousing talk at half-time and we came out determined to narrow the gap. First Mark scored a drop-goal after only two minutes and then we set up camp in their half. Our way back into the game came from a scrum in front of their posts. Sale Tevita ran wide from the scrum and dummied to Fuka Kitikeiaho, our winger, who had come in on a run. Then Sale fed the ball right out to me running down the touchline. I managed to sneak in by the corner flag and then kick the conversion from out wide. That put us at 9-10 and we knew we were in with a chance to win.

With about ten minutes to go I got a kick twenty-five metres out and just left of the post following a dangerous tackle. After all the practice I was confident of being able to kick those sort of goals without thinking but this time nerves got the better of me and I sliced it. I thought it hadn't gone over and sank to my knees. Then, all of a sudden, the ball seemed to change direction and sneak inside the right-hand post. The crowd applauded and I breathed a loud sigh of relief.

As it turned out, I needn't have worried so much because Fuka (pronounced Fooka) scored a great little try not long afterwards by beating off two tackles. Fuka was big for a winger and had legs the size of a prop's making him hard to tackle. Come to think of it, he definitely was a big Fuka. Unfortunately I didn't manage the conversion but we still won the game 16-10 and picked up our 'bonus' points.

The third game, our third of the week, was a 'biggie'. It was against Marist-St Pats who had won the Swindale Shield the year before and who had beaten Ories by about 30 points. Clive set about motivating us for the game but he also took a disciplined and organised approach. He and Keith Mettric, the forwards coach, worked out the scrum moves, where to kick from and how to move the back line. It was imprinted on our brains that we should stick to the game plan.

The game was at held Athletic Park and it was Ories first feature game for 12 years (a feature game was the adjudged 'best prospect' of an exciting game in the league for the week and therefore held at the provincial ground). We managed to keep to our game plan for the whole match but Marists were just that bit too strong for us. It showed in the teams. Our tallest player was Ash Pointen at about 6' 4" whilst their tallest was a massive 6' 8". The difference was also evident in the scrums where they were about a stone heavier per man. In addition the Marists had a very experienced half-back in Neil Sorenson who was the provincial half-back at the time.

My first penalty attempt after about 30 minutes fell short but ended up with us pressuring the Marists line. Richard Brookie, our No.8, managed to fight his way over for a try which I converted to give us a sniff of a chance. However they managed to put more points on the board than us and we went in at half-time trailing by 14-6.

In the second half, we fared a bit better with me scoring two penalties and Mark getting another of his drop-goals but we came off eventual losers by 21-15. Several people said that they thought we were unlucky to lose because we had hassled Marists and put them off their game. Whether it was true or not, we had given Marists a scare and started the season very well.

After that hectic first week to the season we had a bit of a rest until our fourth game against Western Suburbs. A whole six days off if you don't include training. We won it by 24-16 with me picking up two tries, one conversion and a penalty.

That third victory from four games put us into third place in the league behind Wellington and MSP. It also put a smile on Clive's face. I was none too miserable either, my start to the season had been as happy and as unexpected as Ories' had. It made me begin to realise that I could at least hold my own and I wasn't going to be completely out-classed. My sense of relief was enormous and I started to enjoy myself because I felt that I wasn't going to let anybody down.

The press rightly put Ories good start down to our coaches. If you lined our players up side-by-side with the opposition before a game you would have always called us the under-dogs. The difference was our teamwork and the patterns that Clive and Keith had taught us. They had drilled us until we knew exactly what to do. In addition to good playing skills they had also developed a healthy attitude within the team which helped us to generate a fantastic team spirit.

There was a fair bit of competition for places, apart from full-back. The hardest position to make your own was loose-forward because there were quite a few good players around who could fill that spot. Although everybody wanted to get into the team, the rivalry was very friendly and nobody held a grudge if he was left out. I was fairly confident of holding my place because of the lack of full-backs and because I had risen to the top of the point-scorers table. After four games, I led with 48 points, seven ahead of Mark Gray who played for University and eleven ahead of Wayne Gray who played for Marists. It was a bit of a surprise, but I was fairly proud and sent a batch of cuttings back home to everyone I knew.

I'd also noticed in the papers that I had been awarded some points in the Billy Wallace Trophy. Billy Wallace had been a great All Black and Wellington player. When he died a memorial trophy was instigated by the Wellington Union for the best and fairest club player of the year. Points were awarded in each game of the season, three to the best player, two to the second best and one to the third best. Journalists assessed each game and I was awarded three points for my part in Ories win over WCOB. The cutting simply said "John Gallagher, Oriental full-back. Joined the backline well and kicked well judged goals". It wasn't a lot, but it was worth a million to me.

Because of my encouraging start for Ories the press also began to develop a small interest in me. One paper asked me to do a short interview and quizzed me on the differences between rugby in New Zealand and Great Britain. I had noticed in the few games in which I'd played that the general tempo was higher. This meant that more breaks got through and I had to do more tackling. I think the greater pace of games was due to the higher fitness levels of players in New Zealand; though I must stress that this is only at the standard of rugby which I was playing at the time. Players in Britain seemed to play rugby to get fit, whilst players in New Zealand seemed to get fit to play rugby. There was a whole different attitude to training in general and to pre-season training in particular. In addition I noticed the ball was coming out wide more often than I had been used to. In Britain, the ball would come out to the stand-off who would kick, leading to a 'kick-and-chase' game. In New Zealand, they would throw the ball out to the wings whenever possible, leaving an overlap for incoming players such as the full-back (Clive always wanted me to join the line as much as possible).

When the interview was printed it came out under the heading "Hullo 'ullo ... Ories' new man is no plodder" and they kept referring to me as 'London Bobby' ! Naturally I bought lots of copies to send back home. I even sent one to my recruitment officer in the police force to show him that I was still serious about coming back to join up.

Chapter 5

While the Cat's Away

Petone was one of the three clubs which traditionally battled it out for the Swindale Shield and Jubilee Cup along with Wellington (the club side, not the province) and Marist-St Pats. After an important game against Poneke in terms of local rivalry, which we won 13-9, we prepared for the 'big' game against Petone, which was more important in terms of the league. By the fifth game, Ories was in third position behind Wellington, MSP and level with Petone. More significantly, I was going to be playing against Allan Hewson who was the resident All Black full-back. The only time that I had seen Allan play was on the TV when the All Blacks had beaten the British Lions in all four tests the previous year. Competing against him was going to be one of the biggest tests of the year for me. Although I was a little worried, I was also looking forward to it, to see how I would handle the situation. I was therefore a bit disappointed when I heard that Allan had hurt his hand in a game on the same night that we had been playing Poneke. However, my gloom was alleviated the day before the game when the Petone coach, Andy Leslie, announced that Allan was fit and would be playing.

On the day, Petone proved too strong for us and we lost by 21-3, with me scoring our only penalty. Despite losing, I was more than happy with my own game. I had taken a few high balls and my defence had been sound. Clive, Don and several others told me after the match that I had played as well, if not better, than Allan. Whether they were speaking the truth or not didn't matter; my own feelings from the game and their comments had given me more confidence and I knew that I was no longer 'out of my league'.

Playing against Petone had lowered my points scoring average in the race to be top scorer for the year, but I was still in the lead. I had 60 points just ahead of Evan Hopkin from Wellington, who had moved up into second position with 59 points, and Wayne Gray from MSP who was still in third position with 57 points. In the long run, I thought that Evan would soon overtake me because he was playing for the top team, Wellington, and would get more chances for conversions and 'kickable' penalties than I would. However, I managed to open up a gap with our next game: we played University at home and won by 25-10 of which I scored 21 points with a try, a conversion and five penalties. The following week I scored another 20 points, this time against Titahi Bay in a match which Ories won 40-13. That put my total in the Swindale Shield up to 101 points in eight games. I'd become the first player to reach the hundred points that season, and I was led to believe that it was the fastest ever.

I was very proud of my achievement and sent another batch of press clippings back home to everybody I knew. A lot of that pride came from the fact I hadn't kicked all of the points. I had scored the highest number of tries with six, ahead of all the usual prolific try scorers like wingers and centres. All the clippings said that it was a remarkable feat to be setting a 'hotter pace' than Tony O'Malley who had been the league's top scorer for the previous season. Making a mental note of it, I saw no reason why I couldn't go on and be the top points scorer myself. My confidence was growing all the time and I began to think that I wouldn't mind staying in New Zealand for a bit longer than six months.

Over the next few weeks, the idea of staying longer continued to grow in my mind. During that time Ories guaranteed their place in the top eight and entry into the Jubilee Cup with a narrow 8-3 win over Wainuiomata. It was the first time that the club had made the cut since 1957, which spoke volumes about Clive's and Keith's coaching.

An even narrower victory followed against Marist Hutt Valley, with Ories clinching their two league points in a tight 15-12 victory, but at a cost. The game was very physical, which suited players like Coxy down to the ground, but not our inside centre John Gloag. He came off the pitch midway through the second half with a broken jaw and was taken to hospital. I went along in the evening to see him, and met Don Bond who was already there. While we were both sitting next to John's bed, I took the opportunity to tell Don my feelings about staying in New Zealand (poor John didn't join in the conversation for some reason).

I explained that I had fallen in love with the country and said that I wanted to extend my six months visit. He replied that it was still 'early days' but that I should come and see him in his office the following morning. I nodded my agreement and we stayed with John while he had his milk-shake, then left.

Next morning I went along to Don's office in the Department of Labour as arranged. He sat me down and gave me a list; "Look at that," he said, "and tell me if there is anything on it that you can do". It was a list of occupations which the New Zealand government wanted from possible immigrants. There were things like Nuclear Physicist and Brain Surgeon on it but nothing that I could do.

"No, I don't think I could do any of these," I replied honestly.

"But you still want to stay," retorted Don.

"Yes," I said.

"Well, there is a little clause at the bottom," he said pointing to the list, "which says 'Other'". I looked a bit quizzical and waited for him to carry on.

"Anybody who wants to qualify under 'Other' has to be a very special case. They need to have an excellent reason for wanting to stay, such as being a top sportsman. Now, you have done very well so far. You are the top scorer in the Wellington league but it is still not a particularly high standard nationally and you wouldn't qualify on just that. However, I've heard a couple of rumours that Ian Upston, the Wellington representative side selector and coach, may want you for Wellington's tour to South Island. If you get in the side and if you do well, there *may* be a case for letting you stay under 'Other'. So it's all up to you, John, I can't help you !". I left his office not knowing if I should be happy or sad. At least I knew the score; either I made my mark at representative level or I would go back to the Met Police in London.

I tried not to get my hopes up about being selected for Wellington because, after all, Don had only heard rumours. Despite my efforts I found myself getting more agitated and worked up about it. I knew that the All Blacks were away on tour in Australia and if I couldn't get picked with them all away then I never would get picked.

A couple of weeks later I was in the Wellington Rugby Union office to collect some messages about my school coaching job. While I was there Mrs Buchanan, the Union Secretary's assistant told me that the Secretary had something important to tell me. I breezed along to his office to see what it was, and he said that I might want to look at the list in his hand. I thought 'hang on, Don's already done this routine', but I took a look all the same. The top line said "The Wellington Representative 'A' Team to tour the South Island (including fixtures against Southland and Otago)". Just below was a list with my name on top. My first reaction was one of euphoria before some caution crept in. I asked the Secretary if it was a joke but he stoically claimed that it wasn't.

My selection was confirmed in the papers that evening. It said I'd been chosen as a utility back and that the first training session for the whole squad was going to be at Petone's training ground the following Monday at 4 p.m. My selection was a surprise to many people because Ian 'Uppie' Upston had picked three full-back specialists in his squad, Evan Hopkin, Rob McCarthy who was the Maori full-back, and myself. The All Blacks being on tour in Australia had definitely helped me get my foot in the door. Not only was Allan Hewson away but so were Mike Clamp and Bernie Fraser, the specialist wings.

I asked around to find out where Petone's training ground was and I took a trip out in my stationwagon on Sunday to make sure that the directions were correct. On the Monday I arrived at 3:15 p.m. to find that I was the first there. At 3:45 p.m. nobody else had arrived. At 4:00 p.m. I still couldn't see anybody and I started to get worried. At 4:15 p.m. I got in the stationwagon and drove over to Petone's main ground in case I'd misread which ground to go to. Nobody was in sight there either, so I drove back again. When I arrived back it was 4:30 p.m. I was starting to get really worried that I'd be dropped from the squad even before I'd even started training.

As a last resort I thought that I would call in to the Petone Working Men's Club, which was nearby, to see if anybody in there knew where I should have gone. When I walked in I saw Uppie stood at the bar with a couple of his friends. Luckily he recognised me and came over:

"Didn't you get the message," he said.

"No, what message ?" I replied.

"Oh, tonight's cancelled, we'll start tomorrow," he answered. I breathed a huge sigh of relief, made my apologies and left.
We ended up training for three nights at Petone before flying down to Southland. During one of the sessions, Uppie got news that his Junior All Black centre, Ian Pollock, would not be able to play in the first game of the tour because he couldn't get time off work. Instead he would fly down later, for the game against Otago. On hearing the news, Uppie muttered something about needing an aircraft hanger for the squad photo with the number of injuries and defections that he had that year. He also said that Rob McCarthy would take Ian's place, that I'd be put on the right wing and that he'd like me to assume the kicking duties. With that vote of confidence, I was a happy man on the short flight to Southland.

Conditions turned out to be perfect for the game. But despite this, we played a static game and kicked for touch most of the time. Although unglamorous, the tactics paid off because we had two good locks in Gerard Wilkinson and Brendon 'Compost' Gard'ner who shut out Southland 31-16 in the lineouts. However, my personal impression at the start of the game was of everything being played at a much greater tempo than any of the Ories club matches. It also had a harder physical aspect with some pretty tough tackling.

Our half-back, Peter Barlow, broke the deadlock with a try in the 36th minute. I missed the conversion and the score stayed at 4-0 in our favour until half-time. In the second half, Tim Perez scored our second try with a kick through on the left wing before Peter scored another following a break from Dirk Williams; I converted both tries. Southland's only response was a penalty in the 63rd minute, to give Wellington their first win in Invercargill since 1970 by 16-3.

That night, because there were a lot of new faces in the team, the older players decided to have a Court Session. One of them was made The Judge and the others assumed a Jury rôle. Anybody who was found guilty of a misdemeanour on the tour was made to skull his drink, make a contribution to The Court funds and to offer an excuse. Every single one of us 'new boys' was prosecuted, me for being a Pom, and The Judge decided that we should all stand up and tell a joke.

Les Hall, the team masseur, who was about 4' 11" tall and 4' 11" wide, was in front of me. He told a joke about kippers which had everybody in hysterics. Following his success was going to be difficult, but I tried anyway and failed miserably. When the shouts of "pathetic" subsided, Les spoke up and said that it was about time that I got a nickname. He suggested 'Kipper', so that I'd always remember at least one good joke. I thought that it was pretty stupid, but the others liked it because of Les' joke and the fact I'd been sleeping a lot. In addition, the player who I'd replaced in the Wellington side was Jamie Salmon who had been given the nickname 'Trout', so the fish connection fitted perfectly.

I still remained unconvinced and decided to take the 'no-reaction' approach in the hope that they would all forget about it. It worked; after being called Kipper all evening, the next day I only heard it a couple of times and then hardly at all. Unfortunately, after we returned to Wellington, there was a piece in one of the local papers by Ian Gault which made reference to the name Kipper Gallagher. One or two of the lads at Ories picked up on it and before I knew it everybody was calling me Kipper. And it has stuck with me ever since.

The evening before the second game of our tour, against Otago in Dunedin, we were having a meal when Uppie pulled me to one side. He asked me about my U.K. situation and what I was intending to do in the future. I thought his actions a bit odd, because I'd been told Uppie was a man of few words. Apparently the only way I was going to know if I'd played well in his eyes was if I was picked for the next game. Being suspicious, in a hopeful way, I inquired as to why he was asking. He replied that he needed to know about players' availability for forming a good basis to the team in the future. He then added I was no good to him if I was going to disappear at the end of the season and never be seen again. No doubt the number of defections had affected his view of stability in the team.

Eager to please, I told him all about my meeting with Don Bond and my desire to stay in New Zealand. In fact, I think I went over the top and told him how keen I was to stay in three different ways. I desperately wanted him to be in no doubt, because if he continued to pick me for Wellington I knew I'd have a greater chance of being accepted under Don Bond's 'Other' category. He listened to what I had to say in silence, but he must have believed my intentions because I was picked for the team to face Otago.

The game itself didn't go Wellington's way and we lost 20-15. Otago's flankers proved better than Southlands' and they matched our own in the lineouts. In addition, they made better use of any ball whenever they won it, making a sound platform on which to launch numerous attacks. My personal game was better because I became more involved in the back-line play when the ball was thrown out. I also kicked four out of my five goal attempts to give me a total of 11 points.

Uppie was bitterly upset that we had lost and said how he needed his top players back for the next game against Wairarapa-Bush. However, he was aware that the game was scheduled for just two days after the All Black's return and he didn't think that the players would want to go straight into an important game. Any chance of me staying in the team rested on which All Blacks would make themselves available, what Uppie thought of my performances during the tour of South Island and whether he thought that I was totally committed to staying in New Zealand.

If anyone asked, I told them that I didn't expect to be picked, even though I desperately wanted to be. Deep down I thought my chances were low; two wingers and a full-back were returning which only left one centre place 'unclaimed'. Despite the fact that I had played most of my games in Britain at centre, Uppie hadn't given me a run in that position and didn't know what I could do.

The full squad of twenty players was named about a week before the game, which was still a few days before the All Blacks return, and I was in it. Of course I thought my inclusion was great, but I realised no indication had been given as to which players would make up the eventual playing team. However, when the internationals finally set foot on New Zealand soil, Uppie found out that Bernie Fraser, the left wing, was injured. Bernie's bad luck turned into my good luck and I was picked to fill his spot.

In the game itself, the returning players made a lot of difference to Wellington's strength but we were still restricted to a narrow 29-23 win. I wasn't at all happy with my game and spent the whole match running around like a headless chicken. Allan Hewson returned at full-back and he did all the kicking, so I hardly touched the ball. My confidence was blown to pieces, and I ended up thinking I would never get picked again to play representative rugby, especially once Bernie Fraser was fit.

While I was busy trying to cement my place in the Wellington side, Don Bond decided that I had been molly-coddled for too long at the Thurlow's. The time had come, he said, to put me in with a real Kiwi joker and he introduced me to Dennis Fisher.

My first impression of Dennis, or Bootsie, was his size; he was built like a brick-outhouse. When he shook my hand, it totally disappeared inside his. Each of his fingers was as thick as my wrist and his handspan was the diameter of a dinner plate.

"So, ya silly Pom," he bellowed "ya wanna come an' live with me, do ya ?"

There wasn't really any choice or I might have replied in the negative. I'm glad I didn't, because I ended up having a really good time, and living with him furthered my progress towards standing on my own two feet.

Bootsie was a forty year-old bachelor who had never found the time to get round to marriage. He had played prop for Ories' first team and was still playing for the President's XV. During the week he ran his own business, which he had not long started, making trophies. In his spare time he used to go fishing and had his own boat. He had a sizeable three bedroomed house at Island Bay in Wellington with a big open fire which only kept part of it warm, and the rest was freezing cold. It was on the large size for one person so he had bricked up one of the back rooms.

Bootsie was very easy going and used to come home every Friday night with a couple of six-pint beer flagons for us both. He'd then cook some crayfish and knuckles of pork while we chatted about rugby and slowly sipped away at the brew. I was never allowed to use a knife or fork to eat with ("What do ya want those for, ya stupid Pom ?") but I would always hungrily devour the lot with grease dripping down my shirt. Although I liked it, I couldn't stomach that sort of food every day. As a result, Coxy, who had the same sort of set-up in his flat, and I used to eat out a lot in posh restaurants such as McDonald's.

One day Clive noticed how much socialising Coxy and I were doing and cornered us after training. "I think you two are burning the candle at both ends," he said looking at our stomachs, "and when did you last have any vegetables ?". Coxy and I looked at one another and shrugged our shoulders. We asked if the lettuce and tomato in a Big Mac counted, which confirmed his worst suspicions, and he immediately took us to his house where Jill cooked us a huge dinner with loads of greens. When Bootsie heard about Clive's concern he also decided to do something about my diet. He arrived after work with a large cabbage and took it into the kitchen. Then he took out the rusty butter knife, cut the cabbage in two, and gave me one half saying "get this down ya skinny guts, ya silly Pom".

The final Swindale Shield table left Ories in fifth position behind Wellington, Petone, Marist-St Pats and Poneke, to qualify for the Jubilee Cup. Everybody at the club was really happy with the achievement and we had a party to celebrate. Unfortunately our performances in the Cup itself were not so good; we only managed to win one game against Hutt Valley Marists and to draw one against Upper Hutt. After our seven games we finished in seventh position out of eight with Marist-St Pats winning the Cup.

On a personal level, I briefly lost my lead in the points table to Evan Hopkin at the end of the main Swindale Shield series. Fortunately for me, but unfortunately for Evan, he picked up an injury in training which prevented him from playing in most of Wellington's Jubilee Cup games. Plenty of penalties for Ories gave me the chance to regain the lead and to top two hundred points. The final table put me in first position with 205 points (out of Ories grand total of 309) and Evan second with 175 points. My total wasn't all derived from goals. It also included eight tries, of which I was proud. In my first season I'd become the highest ever points scorer in the Wellington clubs league.

With the club season ending in Mid-August, I was due to fly back home to England. However the provincial season continued until the start of October. Don had been keeping a careful eye on how I was doing and he managed to arrange a two month extension to my visa, so that I could continue playing for Wellington if selected. At that stage he had more belief in me being chosen again than I had. My confidence had been blown to pieces after the game against Wairarapa-Bush and I thought that I would never get picked again. I walked around for days in a bad mood and probably got on everybody's nerves, including Colin Nelson Harrington Bridge's.

What I didn't know was that Bridgey would react to my mood. Apparently he picked up the 'phone and called Uppie at the Wellington Union's headquarters. When he got through, he told Uppie that I wasn't a full-back and I wasn't a winger but that I was a natural centre. When Bridgey told me what he had done I became more convinced that my representative career was over and started planning my summer in London. However, the next thing that I knew was I had been picked at centre for the game against Taranaki and I was also asked to take over the goal kicking. Whether my choice had anything to do with Bridgey, or whether I was chosen because of my experience at centre in Britain, I will probably never know. The thing that I did know was that 'make-or-break' time had arrived. The only position up for grabs was at centre and I was getting a chance to take it. If I failed, it was the Met Police for me.

We only had one training session before the match and it showed in the first half against Taranaki. We were playing with the wind and our forwards were winning plenty of ball. However, the lack of cohesion in the back line meant that we often overcrowded ourselves and took the wrong options. Fortunately the opposition made several defensive mistakes and a rather scrappy first half ended with us leading by 16-10.

The second half was totally different despite having to play into the wind. We worked on our spacing and running in the back line, which gave us more time to think and to choose our options. Although I didn't manage to score a try myself, my mind started to switch back into playing centre and I set up a couple for the wingers. Our revised tactics worked well and we eventually won by 40-20. The total included 20 points, four penalties and four conversions all from my boot: and the supporter's club consequently gave me the player-of-the-day award.

My good performance, and Uppie's belief in me, meant that I stayed in the Wellington team at centre for the rest of the season. We had a further seven games including a memorable match against Auckland.

Auckland were playing fantastic rugby at that stage and their team was to form the basis of the All Black sides for the next few years. They'd been winning every game by fifty or sixty points which was unheard of in provincial rugby; a good 'thrashing' was normally by about twenty points. With our defence being a bit ragged, all the commentators were saying that Auckland would beat us by at least thirty points. It was unbelievable, we knew we were having a hard time but we didn't think anybody could beat us by thirty points.

Even our own supporters were writing us off. I remember coming back to Bootsie's house one evening and he sat shaking his head at me (by this time I had become a 'not bad Pom' as opposed to a 'stupid Pom'). He said, "Look Pom, don't be too disappointed if you lose by a lot of points on Saturday". This, coming from a true blue Wellingtonian, was the end. I said, "Not you as well, you're supposed to be giving me confidence". He simply replied by shrugging his huge shoulders, throwing another knuckle of pork down his throat and saying "Yeh, but they're a good team, Pom".

About twenty-three thousand spectators turned up at Athletic Park to watch, and their beliefs of a large defeat for us must have been strengthened when Auckland took an early lead. Grant Fox kicked ahead and a good bounce allowed Kelvin Farrington to score in the corner. Foxy's conversion made it 0-6 to the visitors. However, our forwards soon started winning a lot of ball, especially in the line-outs which Gerard Wilkinson and Murray Pierce ended up winning 27-9 against Andy Haden and Gary Whetton. Such a large amount of cleanly won ball gave our backs lots of options and lots of time in which to take them. After twenty minutes, Bernie Fraser made a long run down the touchline; and a quick ruck saw the ball spin out to Mike Clamp who dived over for our first try. Allan Hewson took the conversion and we were back on level terms.

The crowd were starting to become interested and then got right behind us when they saw that we were adopting an open style of play. A second try for us by Mike O'Leary plus a penalty and conversion from Allan, against a Grant Fox penalty, gave us a 15-9 half-time lead.

In the second-half, Auckland came back at us through two penalties against the run of play to make it 15-15. However we got one back and then Murray Mexted made it safe for us with a push-over try in the seventy seventh minute. A late surge from Auckland gave them another penalty but we hung on to win 22-18. The crowd invaded the pitch and several players were chaired off. Not only had Wellington beaten Auckland but it had been a pulsating match. Afterwards I was congratulated on my play, especially my tackling which had been my weak point up until then.

Living in New Zealand was very conducive as a lifestyle. Everybody and everything was easier going than I had been used to back in London. I was having a good social life. But, more importantly, I was standing on my own two feet and beginning to believe in myself. My pride had taken a complete battering with my 'A'-level failures, and I was only just starting to come to terms with it. I had never experienced anything like my newly found success at rugby before, and I was beginning to think that I could actually make something of my, so far, very ordinary life. Each week I played for the Wellington side I was putting myself up against the best players in the country. I knew I wasn't totally out of my depth, and I thought that I could reach their level within a couple of years. With just being twenty years old, I knew I would have *a chance* of making the All Blacks if I could continue to maintain my form and I pledged allegiance to New Zealand.

However, my main desire to stay was simply because I loved the country. Any rugby ambitions took second place. At first I'd felt homesick, which is only natural, and I'd 'phoned home quite a lot (the calls were always 'collect' or 'reverse-charges' and never lasted too long), but I'd overcome that and started to feel at home in New Zealand.

With so many incentives to stay and very few reasons to return to London, other than family, I'd gradually made up my mind. I was going to be selfish for a change and apply for residency; if I could.

I'd become friendly with Don Bond on a superficial level; he was a really busy man, and I was still an aimless twenty year old, so our friendship couldn't really develop very far. However, he did keep an eye on me in the absence of my parents. Since he was on the Wellington provincial executive as well as on the Ories executive, he was quite proud of my achievements and the way I had played. So, when I indicated, again, that I wanted to stay in New Zealand he was happy to help me through the bureaucracy of a residency application.

On my part, I wouldn't have been totally happy to return unless I could have lined up something in the way of a career. That's where Dave Thurlow helped; he was in the Wellington Police and managed to arrange an entrance exam plus a fitness test for me. I passed both, which constituted about half of the entry requirements, and had a good chance of getting in to the force. Having played regularly for the Wellington provincial side, and almost having a job lined up, it meant that I qualified under the 'Other' category for immigration. I gave Don my passport and it came back with a multiple entry/exit visa. I was as pleased as punch but, obviously, I was still going to have to return to England to sort things out, not least of all with my parents.

Chapter 6

Constable Gallagher

Mum and Dad came to meet me at Heathrow. They had a brief idea of what New Zealand was like from my 'phone calls but they didn't have the overall picture. I couldn't contain my excitement and started to tell them in the car on the way back how much I liked the place. When I added that I wanted to go back and live there for a few years, they showed a lot of concern. Their opinion was that I had a career lined up in England, with the police, and that I would have no family support if I went to live in New Zealand. I tried to explain my feelings as best as I could but they stayed very reserved about me going back. My attitude was also one of stubbornness; I had made up my mind and that was that. In the end, I decided the best way to get acceptance was to let the idea lie for a while.

Within my first few days back, Dad got a 'phone call from a Chief-Superintendent who was tied up with the police rugby team. He said that he had heard I was coming back, that I played a bit of rugby and he would like to see me in his office. Apparently he had read the file of cuttings I'd been sending back to my recruitment sergeant, which was larger than some of the files they had on criminals. Dad was taken aback but said I would go along.

The following day, he took me to Scotland Yard where I met the Chief-Superintendent. I was told I would have a good future if I joined the police, and that I could go far. In return, I was very frank and told the Chief that I was considering going back to New Zealand. He said that he understood, but thought that I would not be making a mistake by joining the Met. He wasn't really trying to get me in the 'back door' because I had already qualified to join the police, however, I got the feeling that his keenness to get me in was motivated more by rugby than anything else. If that conversation had taken place eight months earlier then I would have snapped his hand off in my eagerness to join. But, as it was, I still didn't know if I was going back to New Zealand. At the end of the meeting I asked if I could have a few days to think about it and he agreed.

Over the next few days I took to going out and meeting all the old friends I'd missed while I was away. Slowly but surely I got used to being back in London; it wasn't all that cramped and the air wasn't so dirty after all. Within a week or so, it seemed as if I had never been away. When I thought about my future, I began to think more in terms of security and a job, than of adventure and seeing the world. In the end I decided Mum and Dad were right, albeit a bit reluctantly, and told them I was going to stay in London. I also called Don Bond and explained my situation, saying I was sorry but I wouldn't be coming back.

I joined the police at the next opportunity in early November. Dad drove me up to the Hendon police training college and dropped me off just inside the fourteen foot high barbed wire fence. It looked a bit like a prison camp, and I was to learn later that it was permanently on yellow alert in case of terrorist attacks. My room was very spartan and I unpacked my bags. When I had finished, I only had time to take a quick look around because it was late at night. My first impressions were not too high and my final thoughts as I went to sleep were 'What am I doing here ?'.

The next morning we were kitted out with size ten hob-nailed boots, two pairs of trousers and a tunic. The uniform was made from a black/blue wool material which attracted the dust like crazy. We had to be on parade every morning at about 8 a.m. and our Sergeant would go over us with a fine toothcomb. If he found any specks of dust, you would be given a black mark in his little book. Three black marks and you were sent in front of the disciplinary committee. The only way to get the dust and fluff off our tunics effectively was with sticky tape. We would wrap some tape inside-out in the palms of our hands, and 'dab' at any hairs or dirt that would land on us during the parade (it's a good job that we didn't have to salute).

The closest I ever came to meeting the disciplinary committee was on the day before we broke-up for Christmas. We'd had a party the night before, and I didn't wake up until 7:45 a.m. Jumping out of bed, I quickly got dressed, put on my name tag and rushed down to the canteen for breakfast. Most people ate breakfast with huge napkins over their tunics to stop them getting dirty, but I didn't have time for all that. I grabbed some sausages, baked beans and a spoon to eat them with. Shovelling everything down, it didn't take me long to finish, and I ran out onto the parade ground at 7:59 a.m.

As I stood there, I checked my uniform and thought 'Wow, I'm looking good'. As the inspector walked along the line I didn't have any worries until he stopped in front of me:

"Constable Gallagher," he growled.

"Yes Sir," I replied, wondering what was wrong.

"Did you have baked beans for breakfast this morning, Gallagher?"

"Yes Sir, I did Sir"

"I thought so. You still have one on your name tag !"

Peering down, I could see one solitary bean sitting on top of the safety pin.

"Don't let it happen again," said the Inspector and he walked off smiling.

Classes contained about twenty new recruits and each day we would have theoretical lessons with some sort of practical. One day of the week was given over to sports and another to self defence. Every Friday we had to sit a test on the work we'd done during the week, which everybody was expected to pass. I found it hard to make many friends in the college because most people went home at week-ends. It didn't help that I did the same, because I couldn't stand the place and wanted to get out of there as quickly as possible.

Most of my friends were made playing for the Metropolitan Police rugby team at week-ends. Although I had a good time off the pitch, the rugby was largely uninspiring. I don't know if it was just that team, or whether it was still the norm for English rugby union, but I hardly saw anything of the ball at centre position. It may have been because they were fairly strong in the forwards. There was one second-row forward in particular who was very good, and people said that he was on the verge of further honours; his name was Paul Ackford.

Two games in particular stick in my memory. The first was against my old team, London Irish. It was a close game all the way through, but London Irish edged us out by about 12-7. The second was for the Police under-twenty-one side against an unnamed touring team from New Zealand. It turned out to be the under-twenty-one Wellington club side. When I heard who the team were, I got excited about meeting some of the players that I'd known in New Zealand, and turned up early to the changing room. To my astonishment I bumped in to Coxy; my best mate from New Zealand had been pulled into the touring side as a 'ringer'. I shouted to him across the corridor "Hello Coxy, how are you ?". His only reply was "Ah, ya silly Pom, I'm gonna kill ya" before the Wellington changing room door was slammed shut.

When we ran out on the pitch he came over and repeated his warning but also told me that he would break my legs first. Then, every time I got the ball during the game, I could hear him thundering along behind me screaming his head off, shouting "I'm going to get ya, Pom". Although Wellington won, Coxy never managed to lay a finger on me for the whole eighty minutes.

As we walked off there was some 'high brass' on the sidelines who had come along to watch the game. I was in the process of being introduced to them by my captain when Coxy flattened me from the side with a chest high tackle. We both splattered into a huge puddle and proceeded to roll about wrestling in the mud. After two minutes we were both exhausted and lay there laughing, much to the incredulity of the visitors. Later on Coxy and I went for a drink together and a chat about old times. At the end of the evening Coxy looked into his pint and said to me, "I'm on a mission from Ories - I've got to take you back, Pom". I burst out laughing, but I got the message.

Can you blame me for not wanting John to go back to New Zealand ? The only person I'd met from that country was Steven Cox. He stayed with us a for a while after John returned to college. On the first morning I went to wake him up with a cup of coffee. In his room, I found the window wide open (in mid-winter) and Steven shivering, wrapped only in a thin sheet. He had kicked the duvet and the rest of the sheets off the bed, but couldn't be bothered to get up and put them back on. The next day I went in to find the window wide open, the bedclothes on the floor and Steven shivering on the bed, but this time he was wearing his cap and a scarf. On the third day, I couldn't see him at all. The duvet was on the floor and all his clothes were strewn around the room. As I turned to go out, thinking he'd spent the night away, I heard a groan. Then a hairy arm appeared from beneath the mess, grabbed the cup of coffee and disappeared back under.

Mrs GALLAGHER

Meeting Coxy again made me yearn for New Zealand. My mind automatically associated him with good times and a happy lifestyle. I wasn't enjoying the police college and every Monday I dreaded going back. Why was I persisting with something which made me miserable?

Although I'd returned to the college after Christmas, I still wasn't happy and it must have shown in my general demeanour. On the first week-end in January Mum looked at me and saw that I was nonplussed by my situation, "You still want to go back, don't you John ?" she said. I simply nodded in answer. Then she smiled and said "Well, why not !" giving me her blessing to do so.

It should have been a clear cut decision from there but it wasn't. Returning to New Zealand was going to be a risk, whilst staying in London was the safer option. I continued at the college for another week, but I couldn't sleep properly. Should I stay or should I go ? I spent hours on the 'phone to all my friends, including Kieran and Quinny, asking their opinions; half said stay, half said go.

Ironically, it was uncertainty itself which finally made up my mind. If I didn't go back, I was never going to know what I could have achieved. Staying in London would guarantee me a reasonably good life but the possibilities in New Zealand were a lot greater. My final decision was to go back. I would give myself three years and in that time I would know if I was going to make it on my own, in rugby and in a career.

I called Don Bond to see if there was still a place for me, and to my relief he said of course there was. I then told Mum, Dad, Mike and Pat. They were understandably upset but realised the extent of my dilemma. Mum had already expressed her opinion, Dad thought that I had to give it a go and Mike was very supportive. Pat was probably the hardest to convince.

On Monday 14th January 1985, less than six months after joining, I went to my course Sergeant to resign. When I walked into his office he growled at me for not being in uniform. Then, when he heard my reason, he didn't really know how to react. He must have been on the 'phone straight away because news of my resignation quickly worked its way up the command chain, and I got a call to go to the Commandant's office. In there I got a real grilling; who did I think I was, what did I think I was playing at and didn't I know how much tax-payer's money had been spent on my training ? Compared to the mental anguish that I had been going through, his abuse didn't even register.

Chapter 7

Down to Work

It was a beautiful summer's evening when I arrived back in Wellington. The plane flew low over the bay, and when I looked out the window I could see the open spaces and clean streets that I adored. All of a sudden the stresses and the worries from the previous few weeks just evaporated.

It wasn't long before I was back in the swing of things. I started at Ories with pre-season training and I was given a huge welcome by the players. The team had been joined by Tim Bloomfield who was the latest Pommie import to follow on from Murray Jones, Tony O'Malley and myself. Tim had been brought into the side at the standard position of full-back, which meant that I had to move out to the centre.

I also re-started my application to join the New Zealand police force. There was a bit of a delay while the bureaucracy got itself into shape and then I was asked to attend a medical. It was on a Monday and I thought there would be no problems. However, I was surprised to hear that they had found traces of protein in a urine sample I'd left with them. They said that it was abnormal and that I would have to go back in a weeks time for another medical.

The next Monday I trotted along and repeated the exercise, leaving them another sample. When they called up again and said that there were still traces of protein, meaning they couldn't pass my application, I got a bit worried. Later that day I gave one of the club doctors a call to find out what could be wrong with me. He said that it was probably a result of me playing rugby the day before the tests, since our pre-season games were all on Sundays. Bearing this in mind I made my next appointment for a Friday. They took another sample and this time it passed. The last obstacle to my joining the New Zealand police had been removed.

In the meantime I returned to my old 'crib walling' work. I had been given promotion, or demotion whichever way you choose to look at it. No longer was I helping Bridgey build the walls, but I was helping out at the concrete-pie factory. My job was to move the blocks once they had been moulded, into a spot where they could dry, and then to pile them up ready for collection by Bridgey and the other builders.

I was working for Nigel Goodwin, Richard 'Duke' Ellerington and their dog, Stretcher. Duke was helping to coach the Ories second team and Nigel played for the Ories President's XV. They were both nice guys but it was Stretcher who held everything together.

The noise from the concrete moulding machine was terrifically loud. Cement was injected into the mould and then compressed into shape by a huge steam-hammer, which worked away on my eardrums all day long. There was also lots of dust which got in my hair, my ears and my lungs. When my time came to leave the factory I wasn't too unhappy. Making concrete pies had joined the list of jobs that I never wanted to do again, along with building airport terminals.

The Swindale Shield started again in late March. Clive's aim for the club was to go one better than 1984 and to finish in the top four. It was going to be his last season at Ories and we wanted to give him something back, in return for all his hard work. Unfortunately this time things didn't go to plan; we lost to most of the sides that we should have been beating, not by much, but enough. On the other hand we seemed able to psych ourselves up for the 'big' games against Wellington and Petone, both of whom we beat.

At the end of the season we had fallen well short of our target and we needed to win our last game, against Marist-St Pats, just to stay in the top eight. We all trained hard and managed to dig up another good game in atrocious conditions. It was some of the coldest weather that I had ever played in. The wind and driving rain made it feel colder than some games that I'd played in with snow on the ground in England. Our half-back, Barry Dunn, had to go off because he found that he couldn't bend his fingers. When the game was over we just walked straight into the hot showers with our kit still on. Even though the ground churned-up into a sea of mud within twenty minutes, I managed to kick four penalties and to everybody's relief we won by 18-10.

On the 7th May I joined the New Zealand police force. There was no way of short-cutting the system so I had to go back to college and start police training from scratch again. The college was at Porirua and it bore no resemblance to the one in Hendon. More like a five star hotel by comparison, there was no barbed wire, no constant state of alert and it was set in an attractive lagoon area. Each room was well decked out, there was a gymnasium and a huge swimming pool which gave it a holiday camp feeling.

The training was different as well. We only had to be on parade once a week rather than every morning and even that started an hour later. Another advantage included the uniform which, although similar in style to the British one, was made from different material which didn't attract as much dust.

Normally, I would have expected to spend six months at the college, but the previous year the New Zealand government had brought in an early retirement scheme for their existing officers. As a result they needed to get new recruits on to the streets fairly quickly and they decided to cut the training time down to four months. Towards the end of this period, we found ourselves with a lot of catching up to do. And the new intensity of work meant that I couldn't go and play mid-week or bank-holiday games for Ories. It didn't pose a great problem because Clive understood my situation.

However, the game that I did mind missing was when I got nominated for the New Zealand Colts trials. They were being held at Levin, just up the road from the college, and the police didn't mind me going along. But there was no way that I was going to be allowed two weeks off, to go on tour, if I was picked. So, sadly, I had to pull out.

I would have loved to have been picked and then gone on the internal tour, but at that stage I had to put my career first. Rugby wasn't going to feed me and I was going to need an income. Bringing myself to decline the invitation was hard, but I was cheered by the knowledge that somebody at national level had noticed me and put me in their little black book. I was starting to make progress.

Although missing the Colts trial was a set-back I didn't dwell on it too much. However, the alarm bells started ringing in my head when I was prevented from playing an important game for

Wellington. I'd been selected to play for the Wellington representative side by Uppie right from the start of the 1985 season, on the basis of my 1984 performances. Things had gone well and I had become a permanent face in the team.

My college commitments meant missing one of their games on a Wednesday afternoon against Wanganui, and my place at centre was taken by Bryan Breen. He was an accomplished player who had moved to Wellington and had played for the Counties provincial side. The match went Wellington's way and Bryan had a good game. I knew that he was a good footballer and I knew that he was perfectly capable of stealing 'my' spot in the team. That worried me.

About a month later, Wellington had another Wednesday afternoon fixture at Athletic Park against Otago. If Bryan had another good game it was going to be very difficult for me to get back in the side. I was in a bit of a panic and went to see my Sergeant, Ann Waugh. I explained the situation and she consulted her timetable. She said that although there were lectures planned for the afternoon they weren't really important because I would have covered the material at Hendon. However, she said that I'd better check with the year Senior-Sergeant if I'd be able to sneak away (Senior-Sergeant is higher than Sergeant but lower than an Inspector).

The normal Senior-Sergeant was away and somebody I didn't know was standing in for him. Had it been the usual one then I would have been given the time off with no problems. Unfortunately for me, the stand-in had something against rugby players and he flatly replied "No". I tried a bit of pleading but it didn't work; no was his first answer and no would be his last. To cover his own backside, probably in case I took it further, he told the year Inspector who said that if he had made a decision then he had to stick by it. I went back to Ann and told her what had gone on. She shrugged her shoulders and said, "Well you have to go don't you ?". I nodded and she told me to go anyway because it was unlikely that the Senior-Sergeant or the Inspector would find out.

Full of relief I went along and played in the game. We were held to 3-3 by Otago until the eighteenth minute when we started a surge of 26 points to gain a 29-3 lead by half-time. Although Otago came back at us we hung on to win 29-24. The highlight for me was when I joined in an attack started by Murray Mexted which resulted in me diving over for a try.

Unbeknown to me at the time, the Inspector and the Senior-Sergeant were listening to the game in the office. Apparently, when they had heard my name on the radio, they went straight down and got Ann out of her class to explain what was going on. I don't know what she said but it must have been enough because I never heard any more about it. There couldn't have been any repercussions for Ann either because she went on to become an Inspector within three years of leaving the college.

I graduated on 23rd August with the news that I was going to be able to stay in Wellington. When we had originally signed up to join the police, we had been asked to give four choices of where we would like to serve when we were qualified. I had put Wellington, Wellington, Wellington and Wellington. On the day, there was a minor ceremony where we all had to march around the parade ground in front of family and friends. Don Bond, Mark and Raylene Bracewell and Mrs Buchanan from the Rugby Union office turned up to give me a cheer which was very kind of them.

My first shift was a 'late shift' on a Thursday night, and I was put on the beat with another constable who had left college a couple of months before me. All we did was walk around Wellington for our eight hours without anything happening, but I remember it still left me really tired.

On the second day, we got a call to pick up a shoplifter. Knowing I was new to the job, my partner said that I could "have this one". We went along, I took all the details and duly made my first arrest. To save walking all the way back to the station we went outside to call for a car. I said to my partner, "Shall I call for assistance ?". He looked at me in a peculiar way and replied, "Yeh, if that's what you want" with a bit of a smile on his face. I pressed my radio button and said:

"Hello control, Beat eleven"

"Yes Beat Eleven," came back over the radio.

"Could I have some assistance please".

"Do you mean that, Beat Eleven ?".

"Yes, could you please send assistance to..." and I gave the address.

Within minutes, three police cars came screaming round the corner with their sirens going and lights flashing. They skidded to a halt in front of us, the occupants dived out and asked us where the trouble was. My partner smiled and pointed at me. I said I just needed a car to take my first arrest back to the station. They rolled their eyes, got back in and drove off. It was then that I realised my mistake, calling for 'assistance' means that you are in trouble and it's akin to pushing the panic button. Word soon got round, and I was the laughing stock for a whole month.

The next day, Saturday, Wellington had a game against Counties at Athletic Park. It started very well for us and I scored a try in the first five or six minutes. Then, at 3:21 p.m. precisely, I cut inside our stand-off, ran back through the Counties forwards and up the main stand touchline. Out of the corner of my eye I could see the Counties half-back coming straight at me. I had to make a split second decision; to go round him, to cut inside, to chip over or to take the tackle.

I can't remember which I settled on, but I left it too late. He hit me high, but not illegally, and twisted me backwards. My left leg was trapped between his legs and I felt my ankle lock. Just at that moment the Counties forwards, led by Andy Dalton, caught up and hit us as hard as they could. As we all landed I heard a big crack.

When play had moved away from my vicinity, I looked down and my ankle was at ninety degrees to the front of my shin. I stayed on the ground and the St Johns Ambulance people ran over to give me first aid. Everybody in the crowd was fairly quiet because it was obvious that I had hurt myself. Everybody, that is, except one ignorant loud mouth who shouted out "Get up ya silly Pommie poofta". Murray Mexted, our captain, came over to ask me how it was and I replied, "Not good". He suggested I should "get up and jog it off", but the medics disagreed. I'm not too ashamed to say that for once I disobeyed the captain's orders.

When they got me to the hospital it turned out that I had completely dislocated my ankle and broken my fibula. To stop me moving the lower part of my leg altogether they put me in plaster right up to my thigh. The whole experience was novel to me because I had never had a bad injury before. The doctors said it was a 'good break' because it went straight back into position when they reset it, but there was no way of telling when I would be able to play again.

I had the full cast on for two weeks and then had the top part above my knee cut away. The wastage of the upper part of my leg amazed me. I couldn't believe how quickly all that hard training had gone out the window. There was virtually no muscle left and my skin was all yellow and flaky, which made me very worried about the state of my lower leg.

Over the next two weeks it started to get very itchy around my ankle and I asked them to have a look at it during one of my check-ups. They cut away part of the plaster to see what the problem might be, and there was a whole load of 'gunk' on my ankle. The gauze had rubbed away, leaving my skin in contact with the plaster-of-paris, which I was apparently allergic to. The area had become infected and the build-up of puss meant you could virtually see through to the bone.

When the plaster finally came off six weeks later, there was indeed a lot of wastage. I consulted a physiotherapist to help me get the full range of movement back into the ankle. He made me do a lot of weights to build up the muscle and a lot of swimming in the local bay to strengthen it. After another long two weeks, I advanced to walking and then running in the surf up to about knee depth, which was good for my posture and kept the stress off my leg.

Chapter 8

Finding My Position

At the start of 1986 Earle Kirton was surprisingly elected as coach to the Wellington side. Most people had expected Uppie to be voted in for at least one more year, since he had been the coach for the previous nine. Earle had a good record, especially in England where he had coached Harlequins and Middlesex, winning the English County championship in 1979.

Obviously new coaches have new ideas and usually have a 'sweep out' of players when they take over. Earle was no exception. He brought in a few new faces, the most noticeable of which were the Western Samoans Johnny Schuster and Lolani Koko. Johnny already had a track record having played for Auckland colts and New Zealand colts, before moving down to Wellington and Marist-St Pats. Lolani Koko was less well known but he was like lightening, clocking something like 10.6 seconds for the 100 metres. Neither Johnny nor Lolani spoke much. Johnny was rather shy until you got to know him and Lolani couldn't speak English. (Incidently Lolani was staying with his brother, Koffee Koko, while he was in Wellington). Of the more established players; Allan Hewson had decided to concentrate on his club rugby for the start of the season which left the number-fifteen slot open. I was lucky enough to be kept in the team as outside centre, but for the first few games, I was asked to fill in at full-back because of my club experience in that position.

The provincial season started early that year with the introduction of the South Pacific championships in April. Taking part were: New South Wales and Queensland from Australia; Wellington, Auckland and Canterbury from New Zealand and Fiji. We started rather well with a 32-13 victory against New South Wales in our first game. But that's when the team got another shake-up, this time not of Earle's doing. Following the cancellation of the official All Black tour of South Africa, an unofficial tour was arranged. The rebel team called themselves the Cavaliers but were, essentially, the existing All Blacks. Their departure affected the Wellington side with the loss of Scott Crichton, Murray Mexted, Mike Clamp, Murray Pierce and Bernie Fraser.

A lot of other teams were also affected and it started the whole of New Zealand debating the pros and cons of the tour. A lot of the All Blacks had been looking forward to touring to South Africa when it was still going to be official. To have such a potential experience snatched away from them by a court injunction had made most of them so desperately disappointed that they decided to go anyway.

I, for one, didn't begrudge them going when they decided to ignore the ban. If I had been put in the same situation, I would have had to think about it for a long time, but I probably would have gone with them. I'd heard both sides of the arguments for and against sporting sanctions against South Africa but that's all they were to me - arguments. I hadn't been myself and I hadn't seen what people were talking about, so I would have gone to form my own opinions.

Anti-apartheid campaigners say that taking sport, especially Rugby Union, away from South Africa really hurts. Perhaps that's true, but apartheid is politics and rugby is sport. I think it's lamentable that the Springboks and the All Blacks, the two best Rugby Union teams in the world at the time, couldn't face one another. The whole idea of test matches are to 'test' one team against another and see which is the best. Unfortunately, now we will never know which of those great teams was the better. The Cavaliers narrowly lost the 'test' series because the backs couldn't match the power of the forwards. But this may have been due to some missing players or the effect of a strenuous programme on a depleted squad.

The Cavaliers' departure left Earle with some problems, particularly up front. The resulting new side had very few experienced players and the average age was very low, about twenty-three. Nevertheless, we were determined to show that we could pull together and play some good rugby.

Our second game in the South Pacific Championships was against Queensland and we only lost narrowly, by about one point in seventeen. Then some bad luck in our next few games meant we finished the championship with only two wins out of five. However, we hadn't lost any of the games catastrophically and, with so many top players missing, it augured well for the future.

I was pleased with my performance at full-back but I was very keen to resume my role at centre. I still felt as if I knew the defensive lines and positional play of a centre much better than I did those of a full-back. Having spent two years at provincial level trying to perfect my play in the position, I knew I'd been fairly successful. It might have been pompous, but I thought higher honours weren't far round the corner and I would have been a liar if I'd said I wasn't thinking about the All Blacks. The press had also been tipping me to progress which, coming on top of my aborted selection for the New Zealand Colt trials, had made me quite hopeful.

The first home test match of the year against France was rapidly approaching. With the thirty or so top players in the country ineligible because of their commitments in South Africa, I was keeping a close eye on events. Two trials had been arranged between 'Probables' and 'Possibles' from which the team would be picked. I was hopeful of making one of the teams because I could fit in at either centre, full-back or winger.

I was on duty the afternoon the teams were due to be named. It was pouring down with rain, which gave me a good excuse to step into a few shops and see if they had a radio on. Eventually, I found one that did and stood talking by the check-out until the announcement came over. The main teams were given first and my name wasn't amongst them. There was still a chance of being named in the reserves, so I continued to listen but was still disappointed.

I went back outside and just plodded around in the rain. I was as miserable as the weather. It was as if my entire set of future plans had just gone down the drain with the rainwater. If I couldn't make the top forty players with the top thirty away, in other words the top seventy players in New Zealand, then it was all over.

Lots of reasons for not being picked went through my mind including me being English, but what I hadn't realised was I had stopped concentrating on playing rugby. My own hopes and all the newspaper articles had caused me to think about the consequences of each match rather than to get on with the game in hand.

Looking back, it was probably the best thing that could have happened to me. It made me forget about the All Blacks because

I thought that I would never have another chance of getting a place. With my hopes gone I was able to refocus on my technique and get better that way. The result was that 1986 saw the biggest improvement in my rugby.

At the time of my non-selection, however, I didn't see it quite that way and I subconsciously blamed Earle. Just before the teams were due to be announced I had been made aware that Brian Lochore, the All Blacks' selector, was due to come and watch myself and a few others play for Wellington against Wanganui. Allan Hewson had made himself available again for the full-back position, and Earle had put me on the left wing. It being three years since I had played in that position, I had a very ordinary game. I could not help but think if I'd been in my 'own' position at centre then maybe I would have swung one of the places my way.

The disappointment and uncertainties were still rife inside me when Earle called me at my flat.

"How ya doing, Galls ?" He started.

"Well I want to get something off my chest if I can Earle," I replied.

"What's that then Galls ?" he said.

"I haven't been enjoying my rugby recently and I think that it's because I've been playing in too many positions," then, in case I was burning my bridges, I continued, "I'll play in any position for Wellington but you won't get the best out of me unless you play me constantly at either centre or full-back, not both". I'd tried hard not make my voice sound as if it were an ultimatum, because it wasn't. Thankfully Earle took it the right way and, after a pause, said that he would try to do something about it.

Our next game was against the New Zealand colts who were touring the country. Earle called me up and said that he was putting Allan Hewson at full-back and me at centre. He added that if I played well, then the position was mine to keep for the rest of the season. The match came and went, Wellington won 52-6 and I had a good game. Everything seemed sweet and I was looking forward to getting down to some enjoyable rugby in the one position. Then, the week before Wellington's first game in the National championship, Allan Hewson turned up with a calf injury which he'd sustained in a club match. Earle turned to me and said "Galls, I know you'll think I'm doing this to you on purpose but I'm playing you at full-back". I didn't have much choice but I agreed anyway because it was understandable and I didn't really mind.

That first match was against Otago and we won 30-6 with me having a sound game. The second was against Auckland who were the favourites to win the National championship. Allan was still injured and Earle asked me to stay at full-back. Auckland's star-studded side ran everything at us but our defence was magnificent with Johnny Schuster and Steven Pokere tackling out of their skins. Not to be left out I also put in a couple of important tackles, both of which stopped tries for the visitors. Our solidity under pressure forced a series of errors from Auckland, and we won by 23-12. I got the player-of-the-day award.

Not long after our victory over Auckland, Allan sadly decided to call it a day as far as provincial rugby was concerned. His calf hadn't responded to treatment and, with me playing well in the full-back position, he had decided to concentrate on club rugby. It would have been difficult to bring in another new face at that stage of the Championship, so my playing position was finally settled.

Those wins over Otago and Auckland, plus another over Auckland, gave us the confidence that we needed to go on and win the Championship. We ended with ten wins out of ten to become only the second side ever to register a clean sweep. Grant Fox playing for Auckland finished as top points scorer with 132 but I came joint second with Robbie Deans from Canterbury on 117 points.

Our victory had come from a fantastic team spirit and a willingness to throw the ball out wide. A lot of that could be put down to Earle's way of doing things. He thoroughly deserved to take some of the glory because he had been very firm in wanting us to play flamboyantly. However, to be fair to his predecessor, Ian Upston didn't have Lolani Koko, Johnny Schuster or Steven Pokere in the province when he was coach, otherwise he too could have formed an expansive side.

I rated Earle as an excellent coach. He always looked for the positive aspects of the game and didn't worry too much about the negative side. Given a choice he would always go for a player who would add a bit of excitement rather than a player who was secure. His entire attitude was; if you made a mistake trying to be adventurous then it was forgivable but if you made a mistake trying to be safe then it was inexcusable.

An open style of play went hand in hand with Earle's character; he is best described as an eccentric with an unbelievable passion for rugby. Everywhere he went he wore a tweed cap and scarf, smoked big cigars and drank champagne. He also carried some sliced lemon in a plastic bag inside his jacket so he could add it to any gin-and-tonics that might come his way.

One of Earle's main hobbies seemed to be winding people up. Somehow he always managed to do it in such a way that everybody saw the funny side of it rather than being offended. I certainly fell victim to his sense of humour on more than one occasion.

The start of the season had obviously been hard with Uppie being voted out and Earle being voted in. I could see that there was a lot of behind-the-scenes cloak and dagger stuff going on but the players wanted to keep well away from it. If any of them had any doubts about Earle they were dispersed when he marched in to the changing rooms after our first game. He proclaimed a "fantastic win" and produced a crate of champagne.

That set the scene for the rest of the year. Whether we won by two or twenty points and be it against our main rivals or the worst side in the league, it was always a "time to celebrate, a win's a win" and out would come the champagne. Mike O'Leary, an uncompromising beer drinker, was quoted as saying, "I was a bit dubious about Earle when he started bringing this bubbly stuff into the changing rooms. But you can get quite used to it after a couple of crates".

During the year there had been quite a few funny incidents, most of them centring around Lolani Koko. He was a huge strapping lad and could run like the wind but he had his own ideas on how to play rugby.

Our first trials for Wellington had been virtually mid-summer because of the new South Pacific championship. I was still playing at centre and Johnny Schuster was inside me with Lolani on my outside. Johnny could speak english but he wasn't letting on to the fact and Lolani couldn't understand a word. I was the 'experienced' player of the three having played two years for Wellington whereas it was Johnny's and Lolani's first year. It was up to me to call the shots and pick the moves.

At one of the scrums I turned to Johnny and indicated that we should do a scissors movement and that he should put Lolani through the gap. Johnny nodded and I told him to tell Lolani. (Meanwhile the ball was going into the scrum). Johnny made some noises, which I assumed to be Western Samoan, and I turned to Lolani and said "Did you get that" in English. Lolani looked at me, smiled with a huge toothy grin and his eyebrows went up and down. I thought to myself 'I think he's got it' just as the ball came out of the scrum.

The stand-off passed the ball straight to me, Johnny ran round, I drew the defence, passed the ball to Johnny who made a half break and turned to look for Lolani. Mr Koko, however, was still standing on his line watching what was going on. When the play broke down I looked at Johnny and said to him, "I thought you said he got it !". Johnny looked at me blankly and replied, "Got what ?".

But by the end of the season Lolani was playing with so much confidence it was almost unbelievable. I remember trying to follow him on a break in our final game of the year. I hadn't got a hope of keeping up with him and he was going to score easily. Then, about ten yards short of the line, he virtually stopped running and waited for the opposition full-back to catch him up. When the tackler came in, Lolani stuck out one of his muscular hands, threw him down into the mud and proceeded to walk over the line !

Johnny and I became great friends during the season because we had a lot in common. We were both 'foreigners', we were the same age and we both shared the same sense of mischievous humour. Although we didn't socialise too much outside of rugby we saw a lot of one another while we were on tour and usually shared a room. After each match we would often go out for a beer or three and then hit the night clubs.

This happened on the night we clinched the title against Manawatu. On the way back, the coach stopped at Otaki or, to be precise, the imaginatively named 'Otaki Pub'. The pub owners had heard we had won the championship so they produced lots of champagne and beer. Accordingly, everybody was very drunk when we left for Wellington. Once back, Johnny and I decided to continue the celebrations and go clubbing. We had a lot more to drink and I finally rolled into my bed at about 4 a.m.

Around 9:30 a.m. I was woken by the 'phone ringing. Having left it a minute to see if they would ring off, I got out of bed and wandered over with a severe pain in my head. When I picked it up a cheerful voice said "Hi Kipper, it's John MacBeth from Radio 2ZB".

"Yeh," I replied eloquently, "what do you want ?"

"Can I have a quick word with you ?"

"What about ?" My head was really hurting.

"Well, I'd just like to tell you that you've made the All Blacks"

"Don't be stupid"

"It's right, you have !"

"Nah, they're not even naming the team for a half hour," I groaned. Even though I thought that I would never get in, I had kept an eye on what was happening and I knew that they were going to name the team to tour France at 10 a.m.

"It's true Kipper, you're in the team"

"You're joking, you're having me on," I kept saying, still not fully aware of my own surroundings.

The conversation went on for about another minute with John trying to persuade me that I had really been picked to tour France and me not believing him. Of course, I had fully woken up by the end of the call, but my headache was none the better. After a strong coffee I switched on the radio and listened for the team announcement, just to make sure.

To my extreme surprise, my name was the second one read out after that of Kieran Crowley. Initially I sat still in disbelief, then I started jumping round the room, my hangover forgotten. When I calmed down I caught the end of the broadcast "...and now we have an exclusive interview with the new cap, John Gallagher...". There followed a tape recording of the conversation that I'd just had with John MacBeth in a semi-comatose state. It was blatantly obvious that I was hung-over and the whole of New Zealand must have had a good laugh at my expense.

Chapter 9

Nobody is Invincible

The chosen team was scheduled to assemble at a motel in Auckland one week after the announcement on the radio. Making the national squad meant that I was given 'free' time-off from the police to attend rather than having to take any of my annual leave. It's just as well because I'd used my entire allowance for the various Wellington games and tours.

Ories arranged a really big send-off for me at the clubhouse with three or four hundred people. The reason was because I had become the first Oriental-Rongotai player to be selected for the All Blacks. Although the Oriental side was more than one hundred years old they had only amalgamated with the Rongotai College in 1969. Clive Currie would have been the first, but he actually made it into the All Black squad when he was at university in Canterbury.

Arriving at the motel was a bit awe-inspiring. I was meeting up with all the big names of rugby and it made me feel really small, almost as if I didn't belong in that world. My feelings of achievement had given way to anticipation followed by trepidation and finally almost to fear of what I had let myself in for. It was like re-living my first flight out to New Zealand at the start of 1984. Had I set myself up just to be knocked down ? As the saying went, it wasn't going to be any good just being an All Black, I was going to have to be a good All Black.

There was a 'welcoming' lunch arranged and I immediately searched out my Wellington teammates of Murray Pierce and Kevin Boroevich to help put myself at ease. However, before the meal started John Kirwan and a few others came over to congratulate me on making the squad. By the end of the meal everyone had said a few words to me, and I was beginning to feel a lot more comfortable even though my heart was racing.

After we had finished eating Brian 'BJ' Lochore got up and said a few words as the coach. He was followed by Jock Hobbs, the new captain. First of all Jock talked about the season that had just finished and then a bit about the forthcoming tour. He told us that he wanted us to forget what had happened during the year, especially regarding the Cavaliers, and to treat the French tour as the start of the 1987 season rather than as the end of 1986.

At the end of the speech he named the various 'committees'. Although it was light-hearted, it was very important for the squad's morale. Everyone was put into a two, three or four man committee with a special task for the tour. There was every type of committee that you could think of; Craig Green and John Kirwan were put into the Social Committee; Buck Shelford and Hika Reid were put into the Entertainments Committee because they could play the guitar, and others were put into the Lurks & Perks Committee. The function of Lurks & Perks was to make sure if there were any freebies going, such as T-shirts or stickers from sponsors, then everybody in the squad would get one.

The committee which everyone tried to avoid was the Laundry Committee. Kieran Crowley drew the short straw for that one and he was put in charge. One of my main memories of France was of him carrying a big black bin-bag full of unclaimed washing around. After each stop, the bag would get bigger and bigger. In the end, Kieran decided that he was going to have an auction at each hotel. He would empty all the unclaimed washing onto the floor and sell it to the highest bidder, with all the money going in to the team fund. If you spotted a sock or a shirt that was yours, then you still had to out-bid anyone else who took a shine to it.

Our send off at Auckland airport was less than enthusiastic. A bunch of anti-apartheid campaigners stood around with banners heckling us wherever we went. I'm sure they could have done something more constructive with their time, because it certainly didn't worry South Africa. The flight took a western route towards Europe over the USA and landed in London before going on to Strasbourg in France.

Non-test matches in France are not against particular clubs or provinces but against 'Select' teams from the whole of France with a bias towards the province that you are in. Most of the squad wanted to play in the first match, because it had been a couple of weeks since any of us had played and a touch of rust was starting to creep in to our limbs.

Although the competition for places was friendly rather than bitter it was there nonetheless. I was sharing a room with Kieran 'Colt' Crowley who had yet to start his laundry collection. Colt was the incumbent test full-back, so I suppose there was a bit of rivalry between us since I was selected as a utility full-back/centre. However we struck up a good relationship from the start and he gave me plenty of useful advice. Many of the other players were surprised at how well we got on together because we were competing for the same spot. But to me, there is no reason why you can't be fiercely competitive on the field and the best of friends off it. Colt never tried to do a dirty on me and I never tried it on him, so things worked out well.

As things turned out, I was picked for the first game ahead of Colt. He wasn't too upset because it wasn't a test, and he gave me a few hints on some of the moves which we had practised. However, the main help he gave was in helping me to relax. He continuously told me to stay calm and that everything would be OK. As a Taranaki farmer from Kaponga, he was laid-back at the tensest of times.

In the last training session we concentrated on ball skills; cross-overs, flick-passes and the like. The last thing that I expected was for one of the forwards to drop his shoulder on me instead of flicking the ball up. It was Andy 'Wurzel' Earl, a raw-boned Canterbury farmer but a really nice fella (honest), and he hit me right on the jaw. I went flying and lay on the muddy ground for a while.

There was I, just picked for my first game in the hallowed All Black jersey, and it felt as if I'd had my jaw broken by one of my own teammates. I mumbled something like "What the hell did you do that for ?", and looked at Wurzel through slightly dazed eyes. It was a mistake. Wurzel called everybody else across, pointed at me and started laughing his head off.

That's when I learned that it is no use 'losing your rag' in an All Black training session. The others started needling me and saying that my bottom lip was starting to protrude. Of course, it's funny for everyone apart from the person that the comments are directed at. But the sheer volume of antagonism forced me join in with them and start laughing, which got rid of the dull pain in my jaw.

Later that evening, back at the hotel, we had another team meeting. We were told that Buck would be leading the Haka because he was a true-blue Maori and was very good at it. Just to make sure that there would be no embarrassment on the pitch we would have a practice in the hotel.

Being the only totally new member, I was pushed to the front by several pairs of very big hands and made to stand next to Buck. He went through it very slowly, but it took me more than five attempts to get it vaguely right. Seeing my worried looks, Buck said I shouldn't fret because I could just follow him.

The game was being played at the main football stadium in Strasbourg, very late in the evening at 8:30 p.m. on the 21st October, my mothers birthday. In the afternoon, Richie Guy called us to his office to pick up our jerseys. When he handed it to me I felt as if I was being given a precious stone to look after. I held it in both my hands as if it wasn't real, turned and slowly walked out like a messenger bearing gifts.

I took it straight up to our room, laid it on the bed and stared wide-eyed at it for a while. Then I checked the corridor to see if Colt was around. He wasn't, so I dived into the bathroom, locked the door and put the whole kit on. I felt like a million dollars. For several minutes I stood transfixed, looking at myself in the mirror in a sort of narcissistic trance. Of course, by the time Colt returned, I was slouched on my bed trying to look cool with the jersey thrown lazily over the back of a chair.

The rest of the day dragged like no other. I was itching to get out onto the pitch and to get my first game over with. Wherever I went, and whatever I tried to do, I couldn't get settled. Colt continued to be a great help, but I don't think he could have said anything to calm my nerves. Several people told me to have a sleep but I found it impossible to nod-off even for a second or two. Eventually the coach arrived to take us to the game. We all piled on and my heart was beating sixty to the dozen. Then guess what happened - I fell asleep.

Walking into the changing rooms, and starting to get changed helped calm my nerves a little because it was like familiar territory.

However, the thing that really managed to put me at ease was pulling the All Black jersey over my head. As I picked it up my mind was saying "This is it. This is it" and once it was on, I felt invincible. A lot of players say they feel the same way; when they put on the All Black shirt for New Zealand they feel as if they can't be touched by defeat. I suppose it's a bit like putting on a set of chain-mail armour before going into battle.

Jock took the warm up and then talked to us about the team pattern. When he was finished, all the players came over to me and wished me good luck. A couple of minutes later, Jock turned and asked if everybody was ready. The unanimous bellow was "Yes" and we edged out of the changing rooms. I would have liked to have sprinted out onto the pitch to hear the roar of the crowd like an olympic athlete entering the stadium. Unfortunately the changing rooms were below ground and if we'd run we would all have fallen flat on our faces going up the stairs.

The game itself seemed to go very quickly. We went 6-0 ahead with two penalties from Grant Fox, but then the French pulled back with a try in the corner and a conversion. I remember standing under the posts waiting for the kick and being pelted by apples, fireworks and old eggs. The French union had given six thousand screeching school-kids free tickets for the game. Some of them must have been as big as Quinny was at school because the stands were a fair way back from the pitch.

The opposition stuck up a couple of high bombs early on in the first half to test me. I managed to catch them all, but every time I was then steam-rollered by their entire pack and spat out the other side. The score at half-time was only 12-6 to us. But then our forwards started to dominate and the backs gained a bit of confidence to earn a 42-6 victory.

I didn't score myself but I managed to lay on a couple of tries. One of them came from a tackle which I made on the French blind-side winger who had broken through. I took him low and stopped his run then John 'JK' Kirwan hit him high. The ball popped out, Craig Green picked it up and ran down the other end to score, so it was a good 'twelve point' tackle. On a few occasions I found myself coming in to the line or running the blind side but the ball never came out to me. It was predominantly an Auckland back line so they weren't used to my positioning, which is understandable. I came off the field fairly happy with the way that I'd played, but I wasn't sure if I'd done enough. It wasn't until other players started talking about particular points of the game, I realised I had actually been involved in quite a lot of the major events.

My main aim for the tour was to play soundly and not to make a fool of myself. I'd started off on a good footing with the first game and I was determined to continue the same way. Getting in to the test side was not one of my short term aims particularly as Colt was playing well and appeared to have the full-back position sewn up. However, for the longer term I was going to need a new challenge and that had to be getting in to the World Cup team. I knew if I continued to play soundly on the tour then I could make the team or at least be close to it.

The next day we left Strasbourg and flew on to Clermont Ferand where I was introduced to the 'Dirties'. If a player was called a 'Dirty' it meant, as I was to find out, that he was one of the six reserves for the game. A 'Dirty-Dirty' on the other hand meant that he wasn't in the team nor was he a reserve. Obviously the Dirties had to stay reasonably prepared in case they were needed, but the Dirty-Dirties could go out and enjoy the night life.

I wasn't named in the team to play at Clermont Ferand and someone called me a Dirty. I thought that this meant I wasn't needed at all, in other words I thought I was a Dirty-Dirty. So, when all the Dirty-Dirties went out on the night before the game I joined them, even though I was just a Dirty. It didn't occur to me that there were rather a lot of Dirty-Dirties. If I'd bothered to count I would have realised that there must have been at least one Dirty amongst the Dirty-Dirties. (Confused ? I was).

Subsequently I joined in when the crowd started playing 'Spoof' in a quiet little French bar. Or at least it was quiet for our first few drinks. 'Spoof' is a drinking game where you have to guess the total number of coins in the hands of all those playing. Each player can have between zero and three coins in their hand. The player with the correct guess leaves the group and orders the drinks, while the last one left has to pay for them.

Time just flew by. It was the first time since coming together that we had been given the chance to let our hair down. Before anyone knew it, we had each downed about ten or eleven drinks and I'd got a skin-full. One of the others must have noticed a glazed look coming over my eyes, or the way that I didn't quite put my feet in front of one another when I went to the bar. They expressed surprise that a mere Dirty was taking on board so much liquor. It was then that I realised my mistake.

When the others declared their intention to go on to a night club or two, I made my slurred excuses and left. Somehow I managed to stagger my way back to the hotel and clamber up to the room which I was now sharing with John Kirwan. JK was already fast asleep trying to get some rest for the game. I slowly opened the door and tried to creep in quietly. Unfortunately I'd forgotten about our suitcases just inside the door, and I fell straight over them making a hell of a racket. Then I proceeded to knock over a couple of glasses in the bathroom before I tried to clamber into bed.

We both had small single beds which were only about two inches apart because of the size of the room. Luckily I picked the right one and collapsed into a deep sleep. I was totally oblivious to the fact that my face was only a couple of inches from JK's and that I was breathing toxic fumes all over him. Just to make sure that I was the only one in the room sleeping, I then began to snore. John played well the next day, but I think my antics coloured his impressions of me from then on, and it might explain why he has treated me like a lost cause ever since.

The tour continued with good wins in Toulon, Perpignon and the Basque region. I didn't play in Perpignon, but had good games in the other two. My performances put me in good stead and I was selected as a Dirty for the first test in Toulouse. BJ told us all how it had been a hard decision to select a side, and Richie Guy did the actual naming. Colt got the full-back spot and Joe 'Bullet' Stanley plus Arthur Stone got the centre positions. After he made the announcement, Richie came to me and said "Never mind Kipper, you were very close". I was astounded. Everybody knew the others were playing well and I hadn't even realised that I was in the picture. Instead of being annoyed or frustrated at not making the team, I was overjoyed at being made a reserve and Richie's comments gave me an extra bit of confidence. I was to cover the full-back, wing and centre positions while the other five reserves covered the rest.

The first thing that I did was call home to tell everyone I'd been made reserve for the test in Toulouse. Immediately Dad and Mike arranged to come over in a bus with some London-based New Zealanders to see the match.

On the day of the game we all went over to the stadium about an hour and a half early, as is usual for the All Blacks. All the team got changed together, and then we reserves left the 'starting' players to their warm-up routines about fifteen minutes before kick-off. We were seated near the back of the modern stands to watch the game.

About fifteen minutes after kick-off, Colt went down with what looked like an injury to his head. BJ looked at me and urgently said, "Kipper, get down there". I ran down the concrete steps in my boots and it was very difficult trying not to slip. I then had to get through the security checks and find my way through a couple of long corridors to the pitch. It took me about two or three minutes by which time Colt was back on his feet and running around. I searched around and found Neil Familton, the All Black Physio. I asked how Colt was and received the answer that he appeared to be OK.

I took the long trek back up to my seat and panted to BJ that Kieran was alright. With half a wry smile, BJ replied that I better get back to the pitch because Bullet had just gone down. I repeated the whole exercise only to find out that Joe was also back in the game. This time, however, I stayed at the pitch side until half time.

The game had been fairly tight, with the French concentrating on scrummaging and us trying to move the ball out. There wasn't a lot of finesse on show but a mild tension had started to build up. Early in the second half, the French took the lead 6-7 with a well worked try by Phillipe Sella. It looked as if they were going to take control but Jock was having none of it. He ordered an increase in the pace of the game at the scrums and the line-outs, which proved to be the home side's undoing. Buck scored our only try with a low dive from a five-yard scrum, and Colt hit a huge drop goal from about forty-eight metres out.

The final score was 19-7 in our favour, but we felt as if we had been in more control than the score showed. It hadn't been the cleanest of games as the fifteen minutes of injury time indicated, but we had won. With the rest of the Five Nations all struggling against France at the time we were quite pleased with our performance. I was happy for the team and that took precedence over my mild disappointment at not getting on the pitch.

The only let-down I did feel was from the non-arrival of Dad and Mike. Apparently they had gone through one of those experiences that are funny to hear about but not so humorous if you are part of it.

Pat was unable to join Dad and me on the trip so we took along a friend called John Kelly. Kelly was also of Irish extraction and had retained the unassuming, relaxed, style of the Irish. Unfortunately, he was also an avid Millwall supporter with years of experience looking after himself at The Den, and had picked up an ability to punctuate each sentence with some rather 'colourful' words. Dad had been a bit cautious about Kelly joining the party, but he had finally been persuaded that there would be no trouble.

The trip was going to be on a luxury coach, organised by a New Zealander called Matt. When we turned up at the rendevouz point, at 6:30 p.m., Matt apologetically explained that he had only been able to find twenty people for the trip, and had needed to cancel the luxury coach in favour of a smaller 'mini' bus. The new bus had none of the reported extras that had been promised, such as a toilet, and the seats were very cramped. Calmed by the fact that there were a couple of crates of beer on board, everybody climbed on and the complaints died down. Introductions were made and Dad became a bit of a celebrity when the Kiwis found out that he was John's father.

Matt gave out the itinerary saying that the ferry would be leaving Dover at 8 p.m. and we set off. Obviously he had no concept of the London rush hour because one and a half hours was never going to be enough to get to Dover. Dad, Kelly and myself had a fair idea but decided to stay quiet. At 7:15 p.m. we were only on the outskirts of London in very heavy traffic. The driver wasn't helping matters because he wasn't taking the most direct route, opting instead for a series of 'short cuts' which caused more delays.

*Meanwhile, the New Zealanders were tucking in to the beer and were blissfully unaware that everybody was going to miss the ferry. That was until Kelly exploded. He had whispered in my ear that if the "poxy, d**khead driver took another wrong f**king turning" then he, Kelly, was going to have a few words with him. Predictably those words transformed themselves into a barrage of abuse directed at the driver over his left shoulder as he continued to drive. Kelly graciously offered to take over and "drive the f**king coach" himself but the offer was declined.*

Armed with this fresh information regarding the state of the traffic conditions in general, and the abilities of the driver in particular, the New Zealanders responded by engaging themselves in some 'serious' drinking.

Before long there were lots of requests for a toilet stop which Matt refused on the basis of their lateness. Unperturbed the Kiwis put their empty beer cans to good use. Amongst sighs of relief and a lot of raucous laughter came comments such as "They're all bloody full", "Gees it's all spilling out" and "It's going everywhere, what can we do". Suddenly the skylights were flipped open and the noxious substances were ejected. The culprits found it hilarious, as did Kelly, but this view wasn't shared by the horror-struck passengers in the vehicles behind the bus. Dad pretended to go to sleep and I sat there watching the proceedings in disbelief.

Eventually the bus arrived at Dover to find out that we had, indeed, missed the ferry. Luckily there was another leaving that evening, so we caught that one. The New Zealanders decided to celebrate their good fortune and made themselves comfortable in the bar.

Upon arrival at Calais our party reinstated itself in the cramped confines of the coach. Matt had been to France before and explained that the French customs officials were likely to be stroppy and everybody should treat them courteously. Unfortunately, not one of the Kiwis understood his instructions. A year earlier the Greenpeace ship 'Rainbow Warrior' had been sunk in Auckland harbour. Newspaper articles had placed the blame on a clandestine group of French saboteurs. It transpired that the New Zealanders on the coach were well acquainted with the reports. Despite Matt's warnings, they weren't going to allow this opportunity to confront French government representatives go amiss. A New Zealand flag appeared from nowhere and was draped across the windscreen of the bus. An argument developed between the owners of the flag and the driver. Pandemonium broke out, and Kelly prepared himself for a fight.

Into this scene entered the customs officials. Kelly shouted, "Look out it's the Froggy old bill" and dived behind a seat. Further comments came from the rear of the bus on the subjects of the French Premier's masculinity and the state of French rugby. This was capped by a loud and persistent Kiwi-accented chant of "Rainbow Warrior, Rainbow Warrior, Rainbow Warrior...".

Matt and the driver were immediately ordered off the bus by the officials and they disappeared into a dark office. All the other vehicles cleared customs and left. I took a look outside to survey the situation; our little vehicle was the only one left in the enormous compound. Time passed and we started to get worried about what was going to happen. Nearly three quarters of an hour later, Matt and the driver returned to the bus. There was a sober silence as Matt stood up to explain the situation.

He said that the bus had no insurance and that they would have to return to England. Insurance had been arranged for the original, larger coach but not for the replacement. Naturally a new torrent of abuse was directed at Matt, and his character was totally assassinated. Threats and

counter threats followed, but there was nothing Matt could do about the situation. After another long wait we had to return without seeing the game.
MIKE GALLAGHER

The second test was in Nantes and I was on the reserves bench again. However that's all that remained the same as the first test. Right from kick-off, Murray Pierce got the ball and was strongly driven back ten to fifteen yards by the French pack before our forwards could get to him. It set the scene, and we knew that it was going to be a totally different game. France had transformed themselves and had us on the rack for most of the eighty minutes. Jock Hobbs received a blow to the head but stayed on the pitch, Gary Whetton hurt his ankle and had to come off after fifty minutes and Buck had to retire after sixty minutes with an abdominal injury. Those two substitutions in the forwards, of course, meant that I couldn't make an appearance.

The game was all over by mid-way through the second half. With so much French domination up front our backs had no room to move and lost out every time. One of the main surprises on the day was that France didn't score more points than they did in winning 16-3. A possible reason was the poor form of their goal kicker, Berot, who missed five out of his eight penalty attempts none of which were very difficult. If those goals, and several missed tries, had been snapped up then our embarrassment would have been much greater.

As soon as the final whistle was blown, I asked BJ what had gone wrong. "How could we lose, I thought we were invincible," I said. His short but pointed reply was, "Nobody is invincible".

Back in the changing room it was like a war zone. Phil Fitzpatrick had a large gash on his head and most players had ice packs on various bruises. The only person missing was Florence Nightingale. I sat down opposite Buck just as he took off his shorts and something fell out. That was enough for me and I left rapidly.

The effect on morale was fairly dramatic. There had been a hope that we would come through the tour undefeated, but that had been blown away in the last game. Whereas the French had improved, we had stayed the same or even got worse. Jock had emphasised he wanted the tour to be the start of the 1987 campaign. As a warm up for the World Cup it looked fairly bad. But as it was to turn out, I think it was what we needed. Changes were made to the team which may not have otherwise been made, and the players who survived were made more determined to win.

The day after our defeat we had a marvellous champagne breakfast to mark the end of what had been a fairly long tour. Everybody was looking forward to going back to New Zealand for a rest and some rehabilitation of the injuries that they had picked up. It was a time to relax, or so we thought, but a particular French coach driver had different ideas.

We had been invited to go to a function with Jacques Chirac the Prime Minister. A couple of police turned up on their motorbikes to give us an escort. They set off at a fair pace and we followed behind in our lumbering coach. Seeing that we were keeping up with the pace, the outriders kept accelerating. Unfortunately our coach driver seemed to be related to Alain Prost and he followed suit. Very soon we were hammering through the centre of a very crowded Paris at an extremely high speed.

No brake lights came on either as we approached the chaos which always surrounds the Arc de Triumph. Entering the mélée and swinging right to go round the Arc nearly put us up on to just two wheels. As we looked out of the back window to see if we had hit anything we saw a rugby ball bouncing about. Then there was another, and another. The doors to the luggage compartment under our seats had come open and all our balls had fallen out.

The driver was so determined to keep up with the police motorbikes that he wouldn't stop. The traffic got denser and the gaps between the cars got smaller but he kept his foot on the accelerator pedal as if it were glued there. I had my eyes closed in terror while some others seemed to have just found religion. Their prayers must have been answered because we arrived safely, all be it without any practice balls, to be introduced to Mr Chirac.

The year of 1986 had seen a lot of changes for me. It had started with me not being sure if I would play again and ended with me touring in an All Black jersey. My main aim of the closed season was to improve upon my fitness. I wanted to retain my place in the All Blacks and become first choice full-back for the World Cup. I knew that it wouldn't be easy, but I had confidence in my ability and a desire not to be second to anyone.

Chapter 10

The William Webb Ellis Cup

Early in 1987 the New Zealand Union sent out letters to the top fifty prospective All Black players in the country. The letters invited the players concerned to some special training camps, to be assessed for the World Cup squad. I'd heard through the grapevine that this was going to happen, so I kept an eagle eye on the post.

Three days passed, and on each one I was left staring at a bare floor or a pile of bills when the postman went by. It began to get to me, and all of my self doubts started to re-emerge. I contemplated ringing the Union to find out why I hadn't got my letter, but I ruled that out in case the reply was going to be I wasn't good enough.

By the fourth day my entire thoughts were directed at the non-appearance of that silly envelope, and I was panicking like mad. In my panic I nearly physically walked in to Jock Hobbs on the main street in Wellington near to where he was working. I don't think we even had time to exchange courtesies before I launched into my main worry, "Hey Jock, I haven't got one of those letters. Do you think they have forgotten about me already ?". He looked at me like a father trying to reassure a fearful son, and said that he didn't think they'd forgotten about me. The letter must have been lost in the Auckland post.

I liked Jock a lot. He was always very friendly and approachable. The concussive injury which he was about to receive, playing for Wellington against Auckland in the South Pacific Championships, was very unfortunate. He was an excellent leader and almost certainly would have been captain of the All Blacks during the World Cup campaign. His encouraging words gave me the confidence to at least try and find out what was happening.

Although the letter never did arrive, it was made clear to me that I was indeed one of the prospective players.

Around the same time, the Union announced the inaugural George Nepia Trophy which would also help them pick the All Black squad for the World Cup. The trophy was named in honour of a famous All Black full-back, who had died in August 1986, and who played in the 1924-25 side who were, in fact, nicknamed The Invincibles.

It was decided that three teams would compete for the trophy in a round-robin competition. The teams would be called North Zone with players from the north of Rotorua, Central Zone from Rotorua down to Wellington and South Zone from the South Island. Inevitably, the Auckland team made up most of the North Zone side, the Wellington team made up most of the Central Zone side and Otago plus Canterbury teams made up most of the South Zone side. On paper the sides were very even and all the players were keen to take part.

As circumstances would have it, Colt and I were again in the same side competing for the same full-back position. This time, however, we both had competition from another player who was staking a serious claim for the number-fifteen jersey of the All Blacks. It was Andrew Macmaster from Manawatu which was also in the Central Zone. The selectors wanted to see all three of us playing but there was an obvious limit to the number of full-backs that Central Zone could play with. Colt was favourite for the World Cup side so he was put at full-back, I was put in my second preference position at centre and Andrew was put on the wing.

Pressure was building up on all three of us to play well and get the position, but again we defied expectations by staying friends off the pitch. The press were getting excited about Andrew and making him their first choice for the place, which didn't help to ease the strain which I was feeling. When Andrew did play at full-back, he seemed capable of kicking goals from anywhere on the park and of scoring tries almost at will.

The press were also enthusiastic about the Central Zone back line, from Stephen Pokere at stand-off through Johnny Schuster at inside centre to myself at outside centre. Some of the excitement rubbed off on to us and then spilled over into mayhem on the morning of our first game against South Zone. I went to see Schuey and Stephen in the room that they were sharing, and started talking about the game. One thing led to another and we ended up having the grandmother of all pillow fights. Feathers filled the air as more than one lining gave in to the rough handling it was receiving. Clocks and other bedside objects hit the ground when they got in the way of misjudged swings, and beds collapsed under the stress of three fully grown children bouncing up and down on them. It all lasted about three quarters of an hour and at the end we were all shattered. Our adrenalin levels had peaked too early, and we were all about to go and play very ordinary individual games in the afternoon.

One person who didn't peak too early was Andrew Macmaster. That first game finished in a 21-all draw between ourselves and South Zone. Andrew scored all 21 of our points. Our second game against North Zone was also a disaster, but this time for the team rather than for me as an individual. We were beaten quite convincingly. The main thorn in our side that day was an emerging flanker called Michael Jones who appeared to have springs in his feet at the line-outs.

A week or so later the Union announced the names of players selected for a final trial game of 'Probables' versus 'Possibles'. Andrew was selected for the Possibles at full-back and I was selected for the Probables, but Colt was left on the reserves bench. The selections surprised me and I spent a long time thinking about them. Had Colt fallen out of favour ? Had the selectors listened to the media and put Andrew as their first choice ? In the end, I decided that the most likely scenario was that Colt had already been selected, and it was going to be between myself and Andrew for the other spot.

This being the World Cup year there was enormous media interest in the trials which were being held in Whangerei. It was decided that the game would be shown live on television. As if all the hype wasn't enough to let us know that it was going to be an important game, they had arranged for the actual World Cup to be on display.

Andy Dalton was the Probables' captain and he had us training very hard before the game. Everything went so smoothly and worked so well that even before the match I was convinced that this was the team which was going to be selected.

Just before we were due to go out for the game I was stood on my own in one corner of the changing rooms psyching myself up when I was interrupted by BJ. He looked me straight in the eye and stabbed his strong forefinger into my chest, “Kipper,” he said “don’t do anything bloody stupid. Just play a safe game and don’t try to take on the whole world”.

The match started quietly enough as everybody found their feet. Then, after ten minutes, Grant Fox ran blind from a ruck and gave me a flat pass. From there I managed to make a break and give the ball to Craig ‘Greeno’ Green who in turn passed to Buck who dived over for a try. It looked good for me because I had made the initial break and it set the tone for the rest of the game. The Probables’ forwards dominated, and the whole of the team played well with me making sure that I followed BJ’s advice. The final result was about 42-10 in favour of the Probables, which was a fair reflection of the game.

The way that we had come together so easily as a team obviously impressed the selectors, and it showed in their final choices. It was usual for the panel to take a few days to think over their preferences but, probably because of the media hype, they had decided to announce the team that evening in front of the TV cameras. Both trial teams and the reserves assembled for a sumptuous banquet at the Grand Hotel in Whangerei. I remember the atmosphere being very overpowering, a combination of anticipation and apprehension. By this time most of us had got to know one another fairly well. Although we all desperately wanted to be picked, I don’t think anybody wanted to see a friend miss out.

Just before the meal was due to be served, Russ Thomas, then president of the New Zealand Union, got up to announce the twenty-six players who had been selected for the squad. I was seated next to Colt on our round table, which showed the depth of our off-the-field friendship. As Russ finished his speech and got ready to read out the names, we firmly shook hands and wished one another luck.

The first name to be read out was “John Gallagher, Wellington”. The next few seconds were a fantastic emotional experience for me. I was ecstatic, everything I had been working so hard for had just taken a huge step forward. I let out a huge sigh of relief and almost every muscle in my body relaxed. There was an urge in me to get up and dance around with joy, yet I couldn’t. I was aware that Colt had visibly slumped in his chair and he was looking as if the world had dropped away from under him. Not wanting to hurt anybody’s feelings, I suppressed myself and limited my reaction to a smile.

Russ looked down at his list and announced the second player "Kieran Crowley, Taranaki". All my emotions welled up again and I felt as if I could show a bit more. I looked at Colt who had been transformed as if sixty thousand Volts had just been put through him. "Oh Great" I said and shook his hand again, this time a lot more vigorously. However, our joy sadly meant someone else's disappointment and we saw Andrew Macmaster looking very dejected. We both felt for him.

The next name that I was listening out for was that of Schuey. He had been unfortunate to just miss out on the tour of France and I felt that he was playing some really good rugby. A hamstring injury had hampered him all the way through the trials, but I thought he may have got the nod anyway. However, it wasn't to be and Bernie McCahill's name was read out instead.

My other Wellington team-mates present were Murray Pierce who got picked and Dirk Williams who lost out to Michael 'Jonesy' Jones. Another who I thought was unlucky to miss out was Brent Anderson. In my eyes he had been the player-of-the-day in the Probables versus Possibles game, but I think he may have lacked a couple of inches in the views of the selectors. Andy Dalton was named as captain.

I don't think many people knew how to handle the situation, I certainly didn't. Those selected were torn between feeling elated at being chosen and feeling sorry for their close friends who hadn't.

There was very little time to sit and dwell on the rights and wrongs of the selections. I only had one week back at work in Wellington and then I was packing my bags again to go and prepare with the team.

That's when things really seemed to take off. The arrival of the other teams started a massive ball rolling which was to get bigger and bigger all the way through the World Cup. An air of excitement descended on the whole of the country. It was just what New Zealand rugby needed. There had been plenty of nasty things said about the Cavaliers tour to South Africa, the loss of the Bledisloe Cup to Australia and that second test defeat in Nantes. A lot of back-stabbing had gone on, and bad feeling had been rife. The World Cup changed it all and brought about a new sense of unity and of purpose.

We assembled in Auckland and began to prepare with several intensive training sessions. Unfortunately, Andy Dalton was to damage a hamstring during one of those sessions which was to ultimately keep him out of the entire campaign. The selectors kept him in the squad, which I thought was a good move because his presence certainly aided with morale. Andy had such an aura and an authority about him that he helped to keep the squad together and settle the younger players such as myself. Even though the history books don't show him as having taken part, in my mind he can claim just as much credit as any of the team. What he gave in experience and spirit was priceless.

With South Africa forgotten, David Kirk was subsequently reinstated as the captain, which I also thought was intelligent, for our first game in pool three. It was to be against Italy with the second against Fiji and the third against Argentina. In addition, the Italian game was to be the opening match of the cup as a whole, and we wanted to make our intentions known. Worldwide opinion had us placed as third favourites to lift the cup behind Australia and France. However, everyone in New Zealand not only hoped but expected us to win, just because we were the All Blacks.

Those expectations put an extra burden on our shoulders. A few people said it was something that we could have done without so that we could have concentrated on the job at hand. But personally, I don't think we would have been so successful without it. Throughout the campaign we were to be fired by the desire not to let anybody down. If everybody expected us to win the cup, then we were going to have to do it. Not winning would have meant failure in the eyes of the public and loss of face for us. It would also have meant a return to the bickering that had gone on in 1986.

Our final training session was at Pukekohe stadium in Counties just south of Auckland. There was a bit of light rain falling and it was fairly humid for the time of year. Near the end of what had been a hard session we were all called together and BJ named the side to face Italy. I was given the full-back spot this time, ahead of Colt. At last I was going to make my test debut and the feeling of elation returned. Jonesy and Richard Lowe were also chosen to make their debut.

It's hard to say why I had been picked instead of Colt. Perhaps it was because the team selectors of BJ, Grizz Wyllie and John Hart had seen me play in the final trial game when everything fitted together very smoothly. More likely was the fact that I had a bit more pace than Colt, even though he wasn't slow by any means. The loss to

France had indicated that we weren't as strong in the forwards as we had hoped. This, and the presence of wingers as good as JK, meant that we wanted to spread the ball wide. My pace was needed to join the back-line as much as possible to give it more options.

My excitement made it hard enough for me to get any sleep that night without any other distractions. However, in the dead of night, around 2 a.m. I received a 'phone call in my hotel room. News of my pending test debut had leaked out to the press, and in no time had travelled right across the world to England. The call was from a hack in Fleet Street wanting to know my views on various aspects of rugby and the teams in the World Cup. I wasn't even awake enough to give him the short shrift he deserved. Instead, I think I answered a couple of his questions and then put the receiver down in the middle of the floor. Some people are very selfish.

My thoughts and feelings when we arrived at Eden Park for the game were very similar to those that I'd experienced in Strasbourg. I was looking forward to playing but again I was really scared of making a mistake which might cost the game. I also experienced the same feeling putting on the All Black jersey, it gave me a psychological boost and made me feel a lot more confident.

There had been a heavy downpour before the game and we splashed our way out on to the pitch. It was a Friday afternoon and only twenty thousand had turned up to watch the game, which wasn't even enough to half-fill the stadium. I don't think many people appreciated at that early stage how big the World Cup was going to become.

The All Blacks hadn't played the Italians since 1981 so we didn't know much about them. Being an unknown force we had to treat them with a lot of respect. It's a bit of a cliché but we were taking each game at a time, and nobody was even contemplating any further than the pool matches. The lack of atmosphere in the ground seemed to spill over on to the players. We had an initial burst of energy as we ran out on to the pitch, but then we just meandered around for a while waiting for the kick-off. Even the referee's signalling of the start seemed as dull as the overcast skies.

We had a difficult beginning due to our nerves, the slippery conditions and the new type of ball. All our practice games had been with leather balls so switching to the synthetic balls, which had been approved for the cup, caused one or two hiccups. Luckily the Italians were also making a lot of errors and it was one of those which led to our first try. The bookies had been taking quite a lot of money on who would score the first try of the cup. I don't know who was favourite, but they were all wrong because it didn't go to an individual. The Australian referee awarded us a penalty try. It was because the Italians collapsed a scrum just in front of their line, as they were being pushed back, and the aptly named Innocenti strayed offside.

Despite our handling problems we struggled to a 17-3 lead by half time with Jonesy appropriately scoring the first 'real' try. During the break we got into our usual steamy huddle. It was decided to stop messing about and take the game to the opposition. Realistically we knew that the Italians couldn't live with us if we upped the tempo.

Immediately things started to happen. Warwick 'Tails' Taylor scored an early try with the ball being moved out wide, and then Greeno picked up a couple. Never one to be left out when there is try scoring to be done, JK decided to have a run and scored one of the best solo tries I have ever seen in my rugby career. Italy kicked-off deep and David Kirk fielded it, he passed straight inside to Grant Fox who slipped it out to JK about ten to fifteen yards from our line. At this point somebody must have turned the voltage up because JK set off. I was on his left and even though he was taking side steps and jinking around, making fools of the Italian defence, I couldn't keep up with him running in a straight line. By half-way I'd given up even trying to stay in support. He breezed his fifteen stone frame past six players and still managed to outpace the Italian winger for the line. The crowd gave him a standing ovation which the try deserved, and it epitomised our second-half philosophy of running the ball.

To rub it in David Kirk took advantage of a little used option to work another try. The Italians kicked-off from JK's try and the ball went out on the full. The rules say there are three options which the receiving team can take; a re-kick, a line-out at half-way or a scrum on the half-way line. Most teams, on most occasions, go for the scrum, but Kirky quickly signalled to JK alone that he was going for the 'line-out'. I think his main problem was stopping anybody from touching the ball, because then he wouldn't have been allowed to take the line-out option. Apparently he had a bit of a grapple with a ball-boy in that respect. As everybody else jogged back towards the middle, Kirky threw the ball in to JK who had already picked up a head of steam. He tore down the right hand touchline with one or two Italians chasing him. The referee didn't know what was going on at the time but when he turned round to see what the crowd were cheering, he quickly realised and let play go on. The Italian full-back eventually got over to JK as he went for the line, but Kirky had somehow managed to stay in support and he received the pass to score. I personally think that JK was in such an insuppressible mood that he could have taken on the full-back and scored himself if he had wanted to. However, it was right that Kirky's quick thinking should be rewarded. Unfortunately every team we came up against after that were wise to the move and it couldn't be repeated.

The tactic of running at the Italians certainly paid off, and we ended up winning by 70-6, which was a record victory in an official test (All World Cup games had been designated 'official' tests by the International Rugby Board). It was a good game to be involved in as my first test match, even though I hadn't scored myself, I had helped to lay on a couple. However, not scoring again niggled at the back of my mind - I hadn't put a single point on the board for the All Blacks in five games. Some people might have said that I had already done a lot to reach the position I was in, an Englishman playing World Cup rugby for the All Blacks. But I'd always wanted to be the best and not scoring, even in a twelve-try rout, made me think I was failing somewhere. It hadn't reached the stage of paranoia but I felt strangely unfulfilled in my role. I was looking forward to the game in which I would finally 'dot down' so I could say, "Yes, I've scored a try for the All Blacks". As it turned out, I needn't have worried...

Our second pool three game was at Lancaster Park in Christchurch against Fiji who had beaten Argentina in their first game. Hit by injuries, and perhaps falsely confident that they would beat Italy, they decided not to field a full-strength squad against us. Although good for us, it was also a bit of an insult. That helped to fire us up from the start, this time we came out strongly.

Before long I found myself latching on to a ruck near the left touchline, and Greeno popped the ball into my arms. As I looked up I could see the try line beckoning with the urgency of something about to disappear forever. Time slowed. Head down, I pumped as much energy as I could spare into my legs. They responded and the line loomed ever closer. Just at that moment my peripheral vision picked up a white shirt flashing into view. A final push from my legs saw me launch into the air and stretch the ball out as far as I could reach. All the time I was thinking that I had to keep my body flat so I wouldn't hit the flag. The impact of the tackle took me slightly off balance, and I thought I was being bundled into touch. Grass then dirt came up to meet my face. Landing horizontally failed to take much of the momentum out of my body, and I scraped along for about five metres. What a humiliating way to miss out on a try.

I turned my head slowly to the right and looked up to see the referee pointing at the ground. I had scored ! At last I knew I could die happy, but I thought I would delay that particular way of celebrating. Time speeded-up again, and I jumped to my feet with a simple grin on my reddened face.

That try meant a lot to me, but you would hardly have noticed it in our first half tally which made the scoreline 40-3. Greeno had got four tries and Foxy was kicking points from wherever he liked. By that stage the Fijians were starting to regret 'saving' their best players from us. In the second half I was to extend my newly opened All Black points account.

My second try came as a result of Tails and Bullet making good breaks. Jonesy latched on to Bullet's pass and sucked in the defence. When he off-loaded the ball to me I only had to catch it and fall over to score, it was one of the easiest tries I've ever had the luxury to get.

The third was almost as simple. Again, it started with Tails making a run up the middle of the field. From the ensuing ruck Kirky gave me a wide pass on the blind. There was a gap wide enough to drive an articulated lorry through, so I just ambled over and touched down.

My fourth and final try of the game was a little more spectacular because I started from our own half. Tails gave me a lovely pass as I came into the back-line. As I sprinted hard down the pitch, I looked for JK who had come in from his wing and was cruising along on my right. Nearing the Fijian line I sensed the full-back was anticipating a pass so I straightened up and dived between the posts. On my way down I knew I had more than made up for not scoring in my previous games. Blood rushed to my head and I tried to make the actual touching down more dramatic by attempting to bounce straight back

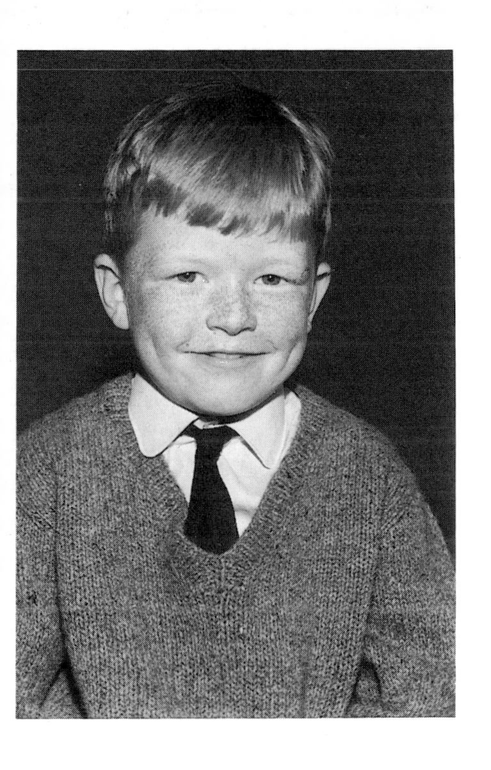

Soccer mad at the age of 5

Bulging with muscle to win
the school sports day

St Joseph's under-12 school Rugby Union team; I'm second from left in the second row, Kieren is third from right in the same row and Quinny is in the middle of the back row.

Top left: In the Metropolitan Police with Dad and Mike; torn between the security of a good job and the chance of a lifetime in New Zealand.

Above: "Get up ya silly Pommie poofta," shouted somebody in the crowd; "Jog it off," said Murray Mexted my Wellington captain; but I had a fully dislocated ankle and a broken fibula.

Left: Enjoying life and having a laugh against Fiji in the first South Pacific Championship; I scored two tries, six conversions and a penalty. (Rugby Press Ltd)

The Victorious 1986 Wellington Representative Team

Fourth Row: Mahanga, Tocker, Gray, Clamp, Barlow. **Third Row:** Williams, Verhoeven, Mexted, Wilkinson, Pierce, Dunn, O'Leary, McGrattan. **Second Row:** Kirton, Schuster, Goodwin, Koko, Frederikson, Hudson, Adams, Me, Crichton, Williams. **First Row:** Lister, Perez, Budge, Boroevich, Sorensen, Bond, McKay, Hall. **Front:** Pokere, Hansen. (Photo by Woolf).

Having a run up the wing during my All Black debut against a French XV in Strasbourg. The game took place on my Mother's birthday in October 1986, we won 42-6. (Rugby Press)

Sprint training with John Kirwan. Having broken my try-scoring duck against Fiji in the 1987 World Cup, I went on to land four tries during our record 74-13 victory. (Colorsport)

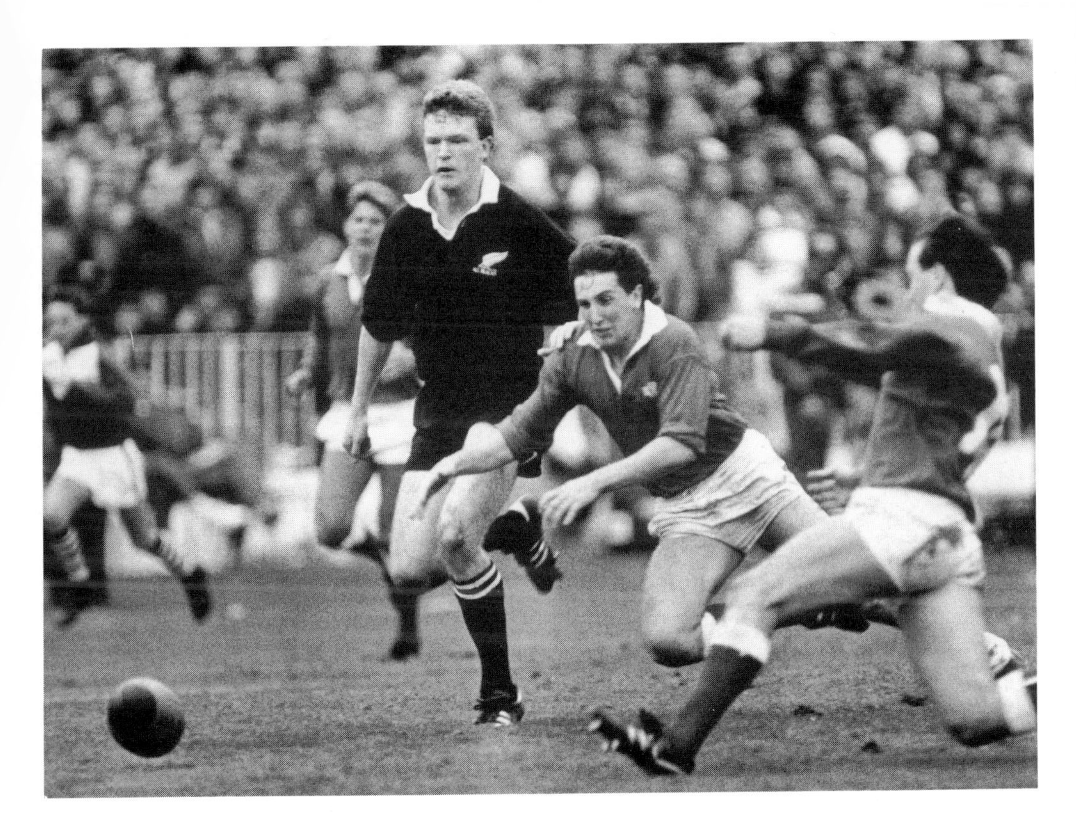

Above:
"You're nicked Jonathan". Arresting Mr Davies in our rout of Wales. He escaped to Rugby League but I'm still on the case.
(Rugby Press)

Right:
Showing some determination in the second test against Argentina in 1989. Good forward play left me with little else to do than score a last minute try. It was my first full test in front of my 'home' crowd in Wellington.
(Rugby Press)

Asking directions from a fan. On the beat with Murray Pierce as a public relations exercise for the police after winning the World Cup. (Evening Post, Wellington)

Looking for somewhere to stay at the Hong Kong sevens. I'm driving the taxi while the others try to fix the spare tyre.

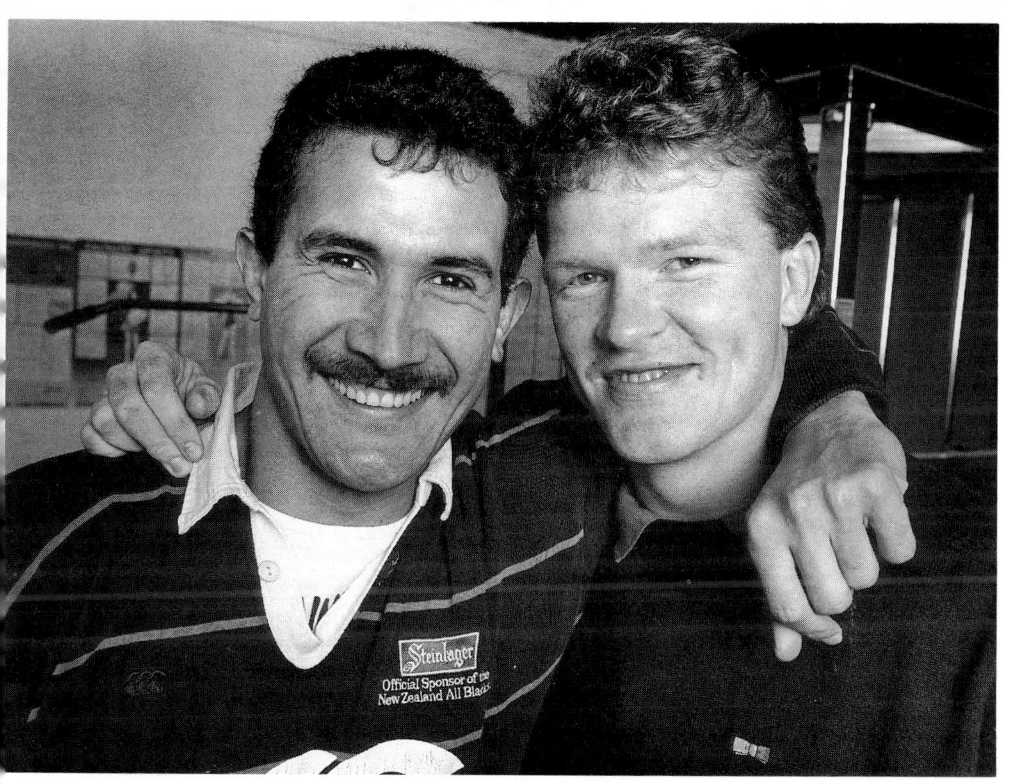

Team-mates for Wellington and the All Blacks, Johnny Schuster and I were great pals off the pitch. My departure to Leeds played a role in his decision to switch codes. (New Zealand Herald)

Carbo-loading at a top restaurant with Frano Botica, Ian Jones and Andy Earl in Cork. Touring Ireland was enjoyable and peaceful, away from media hassle. (Cork Examiner)

Grizz Wyllie congratulates Foxy on another excellent kicking performance in our 34-9 victory
Cardiff Arms Park. Bullet and I are trying to pluck up courage to complain about the smoke
(Colorsport)

Buck - a natural choice for captain after the first World Cup. His power and leadership up front always set a good example. In the background, I've decided Schuey would look better with a tattoo on his forehead.

Right: Mum became the first woman to enter an All Black's changing room at Cardiff in 1989. The lads let her through thinking she was the St Johns Ambulance lady. (Colorsport)

Below: Being introduced to Princess Anne before our game against the Barbarians at Twickenham. After this game I began to wonder what else there was to achieve in Rugby Union. (Colorsport)

Above: Receiving the first ever 'International Player of the Year' award at the Whitbread brewery in London, 1990. Brian Moore (centre) got 'British Player of the Year' and Tony Stanger (left) got 'Most Promising Player of the Year'.
(Colorsport)

Below: Playing with Guinness, my dog, on a Wellington beach. He terrorised the entire neighbourhood but kept me company.
(The Listener, NZ)

A cartoon by Tom Scott, given to me by Ories when I left in 1990

How big was the cheque ? My move to Leeds prompted huge speculation over the amount I was receiving. At the time, I was labelled the highest paid player in the game.(Andrew Varley)

About to get flattened playing for Leeds against the Australian tourists. The arm padding signifies the arrival of Kangaroo captain Mal Meninga. (Andrew Varley)

I see Rugby League and Rugby Union as two separate games. The art of kicking is only one of the differences. (Andrew Varley)

Right: Another different ball game ? I doubt it ! I've got enough on my plate with the new challenges of Rugby League.

Left: Relaxing at home in the garden with Anita.

on to my feet. Unfortunately I slipped and made a real ass of my self, looking like an uncoordinated lemming trying to find a cliff.

The final score was 74-13 which set another new record to erase the one which we had just made against Italy. Apparently the Italian team were in the crowd willing us to do just that. They let out an enormous roar when we scored our last try which almost drowned out the muted cheers of the many thousand, points-drunk New Zealanders.

The scoreline wasn't the only world's best mark to be set in that game. I didn't know it at the time but my four tries were a record for a full-back in an International match. In addition, Greeno and myself had equalled Duncan McGregor's eighty-two year old record for the most tries scored in a test by an All Black. Not to be left out, Foxy also got his name on the sheets with twenty-six points to equal Alan Hewson's test record.

Team confidence was high after the Fiji game but it was still tempered. We knew that we hadn't really been tested and that our third game, against Argentina, probably wasn't going to provide us with an edge to our mettle, which we were going to need in the latter stages of the competition.

The pleasure derived from scoring my four tries had helped dull the soreness I was getting from a knock on my right leg, just above the knee. It was only a bruise really, but I thought I had better get a bit of physio on it before the Argentina game. Neil Familton had a look at it, agreed that there was only bruising and gave me a bit of a rub to disperse the blood. Not long after he'd finished and I'd got dressed the door burst open. It was BJ who had come down to see how I was, "How ya feeling, Kipper ?". "Fine" was my short reply. He looked me straight in the eyes as if searching for something I wasn't letting on about.

"Are you sure ?" he said.

"Yes," I replied, truthfully.

"What's the matter ?"

"Oh, just a bit of bruising, that's all"

"Which leg is it in, Kipper ?"

"My left, BJ"

With that he clenched his fist and smacked my left leg with the fleshy part of it. It was my turn to do the looking straight in the eyes. He nodded his approval and went to leave.

Just as his hand reached out for the door handle he stopped and turned round. Without looking up he focused on my legs and strode across the room towards me. This time he took a huge swing with his fist and aimed it at my right leg. I recoiled and put my hand down, palm towards him, to deflect the blow. "You're not playing," he said, "I'm giving Kieran a run".

In a way I didn't mind. The problem was that Colt had never, and would never, play a bad game for the All Blacks. It also meant I would miss playing in front of my 'home' crowd at Athletic Park in Wellington. To cap everything, my Dad had been to see the bank manager and was flying down to watch me play. He was due to arrive for the Argentina game and would be disappointed again. On top of the Nantes débâcle he was going to wonder if he'd ever see me play for the All Blacks.

Fidgeting in the stands I watched the new-look team, in which Bernie McCahill, Wurzel, Zinzan 'Zinny' Brooke and Terry 'TJ' Wright were also making their first World Cup appearances. They ran out eventual winners by 46-15, which put us into the quarter finals against Scotland.

Colt, to his credit, grabbed his chance with both hands. He scored a try and made a good across pitch sprint, after fielding a defensive kick, to put Bullet free for a score. While being confident in my own abilities I felt that he was stealing a stride on me by being 'fresher' in the minds of the selectors than I was.

My nightmare seemed to be coming true and later that night it got a lot worse. Walking back to the dining room from the bar with my hands full of glasses, I overheard BJ saying to somebody "Who shall I pick for Scotland, Kipper or Colt ?". I hadn't been taking any notice of the dialogues going on around me until I had heard my name mentioned. Naturally I slowed down and tried to hear more without appearing to be prying. Unfortunately the background noise level was a mite too high, and I couldn't see the other person who was stood behind BJ. It ruined the rest of my meal I can tell you; my body might have been in there drinking and munching, but my mind was a million miles away. Had I come this far to miss out ? Colt hadn't scored four tries like I had, but similarly I hadn't got the big match experience he possessed.

The next day I spent on tenter-hooks, listening in on everything that went on around me. I made sure that I always had a glass in my pocket in case I found a useful wall to stick it against. One place that I certainly wasn't going anywhere near was the physio room. Having Dad over helped by providing a shoulder to moan on. I think that he was more confident of me being picked than I was.

The flight back down to Christchurch seemed a long one with me contemplating events. The team as a whole knew that we were entering a very different phase of the competition. Scotland had been playing well, by far the best of the 'home' unions. Their 20-20 draw with the favoured French had shown their capabilities, and it had only been on try difference that they had come second in the pool.

Training was stepped up all round and we heard from the forwards that Grizz had made them do ninety-odd scrums against an army truck. It was at the end of one of these sessions that BJ announced the team to play the next game. To my relief I was chosen. It meant that I could start relaxing a bit as far as selection was going, because, barring injuries and disasters, this was obviously going to be the team to see out the rest of the campaign. Colt was first, as ever, to congratulate me. Whereas I had supported him in France, the tables were now being turned. It spoke volumes for Colt's character that he didn't let the disappointment he must have felt get in the way of his commitment to the team. My heart also went out to Frano Botica and Bruce Deans. Although they were members of the twenty-six man squad it was looking as if they wouldn't get a game in the whole of the tournament (as was the case). It must have been so frustrating for them to take part in the training sessions and yet not really feel part of the 'team'.

Scotland must have thought that it was a travesty of justice to end up facing the All Blacks in the quarter finals. Against anybody other than ourselves, the Australians or the French they could have comfortably expected to reach the last four. We knew, therefore, that it would be a tough game, and so it proved.

The whole match was dominated by both packs crunching away at one another trying to get the upper hand. Neither of them really succeeded, and it's a tribute to the strength-stamina of all the forwards that they were contesting each ball as keenly at the end of the game as at the start.

Despite the battle going on up front, the backs were used extensively and the overall impression was of a fast and furious game. We had several breaks in the first half from which we should have scored, but the Scottish aggression provided some excellent tackling to keep us out.

About fifteen minutes before half-time, Jonesy made another of his powerful runs down the side and set up a ruck well into Scottish territory. Bullet had his hands on the ball and I saw a gap to his right, so I ran straight towards it screaming for the ball. Instead of picking me out, Bullet opted to throw a long pass behind my back to JK who beat a couple of players and touched down. The celebrations were, however, short lived because the referee called us back for 'shepherding'. On my run through, I had collided with a Scottish defender who was attempting to run across the pitch following the ball. There is no way that he would have got to JK, and I never crossed JK or Bullet's path, so it's hard to see why I was shepherding. Still, the referee's word is final and we went in at the break with only a 9-3 lead thanks to Foxy's consistent boot.

We could tell that we were getting the hard game that we had expected. And, unfortunately, things like the 'shepherding' decision were going against us. Bad breaks of luck such as that can often cost you the match. It was therefore decided that we should try and lift the tempo from it's already high level. This we did and the Scots stayed with us until the last twenty minutes when we started to claim a majority of territorial advantage. Alan 'AJ' Whetton made the break through that we had been looking for, after good lead-up work from John Drake. His touch-down was typical of his contribution to our World Cup effort. He seemed positively monumental in the tight and could always be found in the loose.

I was lucky enough to get our second and only other try that day. It originated again from Jonesy who had latched on to a loose ball following a line-out in our own half. He fed to Gary Whetton who set his long legs in action steaming down the touch-line. The backs who were following, including myself, knew he wasn't slow but we were still taken aback by his outright speed. His run came to an end with a lovely inside pass to Sean Fitzpatrick. Sean, instead of attempting to side step, ran straight into the Scottish hooker who had come up to challenge him. The ensuing ruck went over the top and Buck took over with a run to within five metres of the line. At this point he was held up and I realised that the strength of our attack meant that there would be gaps out wide. Accordingly, I positioned myself outside of Bullet and waited for the ball. Grant Fox threw a nice long pass out to Bullet, missing out Tails. Bullet then had the option of throwing to me or JK. This time he went for me and popped up a short one for me to dive over and score. It had really been a great team effort and had only fallen to me to finish it off.

The final score was 30-3, again aided by Foxy's sniper-like accuracy at goal-kicking. The numbers don't truly reflect the closeness of the game, it would be more accurate to say that we won by two tries to nil. Dad had finally got to see me play for the All Blacks. Not only that, but he had seen us win a World Cup quarter-final and me score a try. People sitting with him said that he had been going 'bonkers' in the stand during the game. However, by the time I saw him the next day, he was a bit more reserved and said "Well played".

En route to the semi-final in Brisbane, we made one of our inevitable trips to the local burger joint where the team-manager had opened an account. Not seeing the notes disappearing from my own pocket encouraged me to order more than I normally would have. Looking over the waiter's head I basically read out the entire menu. Everybody else had a similar amount and I think the staff had to send out for some more supplies.

Time went on and I had made a severe dent in my order, when I became aware of money being passed under the table. Zinny had declared his attention, upon entering the restaurant, to break his own record for the amount of food that he could eat. (This was one of Zinny's 'world records'. He used to make them up and then try to break them. If he couldn't, he would just ignore the fact that the record ever existed). The others had noticed that I was keeping pace with Zinny, and a book had been opened as to who would eat the most.

With the scam exposed, Zinny and I eyed one another's trays and the competition was on. Slowly but steadily we demolished the piles of food in front of us leaving acres of screwed up wrapping papers all over the table. At the end of it all, I felt like a pregnant cow about to give birth. The wrappers and receipts were analysed by the judges and

I was declared the winner by a narrow chocolate sundae. My name was duly entered into Zinny's book of world records, and then scrubbed out again when he decided that eating burgers wasn't worthy of a record.

With the win over Scotland under our belts, confidence started to creep into the squad. The pool games hadn't particularly tested us, but the quarter-final had shown that we could beat class opposition. Wales were going to be our adversaries in the semi-final and we weren't too worried about that. We had rated Scotland higher, and the manner of Wales' most boring 16-3 victory over England in their quarter-final hadn't caused us to lose much sleep. Adding to this the fact that Scotland had drawn with France and we began to think, for the first time, that we could win the whole tournament. I wouldn't say that we had grown over-confident but we certainly had a self-belief. In the back of everybody's mind was the fear of losing and of letting people down. That was more than enough to temper our faith.

One drawback we were going to have to face in the semi-final was the fact that we were going to have to play in Australia, at Ballymore in Brisbane. Huge home support was something that we had become used to with twenty to thirty thousand watching all our previous matches. Was it going to make a difference if we needed to lift ourselves for a final push ? Fortunately we need not have worried. When we landed at Brisbane airport it could have been Auckland or Wellington. There were Kiwi's as far as the eye could see. It seemed as though every New Zealander who lived in the Brisbane or Sydney areas had come to greet us.

It was much the same when we walked out onto the pitch for the game. Looking around the stands they simply appeared to be engulfed in a sea of black with one or two splatterings of red. The huge local ex-pat support had been bolstered by an equally large travelling contingent. Final figures for the crowd numbers showed that there were twenty-two and a half thousand watching our semi, as against only seventeen and a half watching the Australian semi in Sydney.

Our pre-match confidence was necessarily talked down in the dressing rooms. Although they hadn't been on-form, the Welsh still had to be respected. Certainly it wasn't going to be as easy as someone thought when they jokingly put up 90-0 to the All Blacks on the score-board.

It might not have seemed that way to start with. Our previous games had commenced slowly and then we had stepped up the tempo in the second half. This time we started aggressively to accumulate 24 points in just as many minutes. I had to keep looking up at the board to make sure that it was real. Buck and AJ dominated in the forwards, while Mark Brooke-Cowden acquitted himself well as stand-in for Jonesy, who didn't want to play on a Sunday. JK was again on form, and Wales had a problem coping with him running at them from every position on the pitch. He also provided a couple of great cover tackles; one I remember in particular was when he stormed over from his wing to tackle Ieuan Evans who had broken away, and everybody else thought a score was inevitable.

Our forward domination was so great that I remember the Welsh pack being pushed a full thirty metres back when they had gained a position under our posts. In such a climate it is difficult for those on the receiving end to keep their heads. One Welsh player, Huw Richards, nearly lost his, literally. He was seen raining blows on Gary Whetton in a ruck. Not keen on this treatment of his team-mate, Buck came over and laid Richards out on the floor. The incident ended up with the hapless Richards being woken up and then sent for an early bath by Kerry Fitzgerald the Australian referee.

Our ascendency up front also meant the loose forwards could stand off the rucks, and that gave less room in the back line. As a result there were very few gaps in the line for me to join in. In addition, the Welsh were standing flat on us, making it difficult to run the ball wide. This showed with Bullet's and one of JK's tries, both of which were scored by running back inside, rather than by going outside.

My part in the points scoring was therefore limited on this occasion. I was left to concentrate on the bread and butter of full-back play, that of positioning myself properly to cover breaks and kicks, and to make every one of my tackles count.

The final score was 49-6 in our favour. A lot of people were disappointed with the way that Wales performed against us and thought that they could have done better. Their subsequent defeat of Australia showed that they were, indeed, capable of some good rugby. In spite of that, I think the scoreline was a fair reflection of the way that we had taken their game apart. If we had been as rampant in the rest of the game as we had been in the first twenty-five minutes, then we could have possibly reached a similar score to those we had made against Italy and Fiji.

During the game, I'd taken a bit of a knock which was to give me an inhibited run-up to the final. Jonathan Davies had sent up a bomb to test me. As I came down with it I was hit by two onrushing Welsh players, one of them taking me high and one taking me low. During the tackle I felt a knee strike the side of the top of my leg quite hard. With adrenalin coursing through my veins I hadn't felt it too badly on the pitch. However, when I went to get out of bed the next day, I found that I could hardly walk and there was a lot of swelling in the area of the impact.

There were only six days before the final and it took four of them before I could run again. I had about three sessions with the physio every day for some very painful 'frictions' and tried to rest it as much as possible. This time BJ didn't come along and give me a clout on it, instead he seemed as concerned as I was about me being fit for the final.

Critics never see the endless nights spent practicing drills in the rain or experience the repetitiveness of trying to perfect a good kicking action. They don't have to come home at night and nurse their recently acquired bruises nor go through the anxiety of preparing for a big game. Incidents such as having to miss out on the New Zealand Colts trials and passing protein in my samples may seem trivial. But, to me, at the time, they were major causes for concern. That dead-leg was a similar situation; would I make the final or wouldn't I ?

Imagine my relief when I finally got back into training on the day before the final. Full movement had returned to the leg but it was still jarring as I ran. A final session of biting my fist as Neil Familton kneaded his skilful knuckles into the scar tissue seemed to do the trick, and I was passed fit.

Interest in the World Cup had become huge by this stage. Everybody in New Zealand, and possibly around the world, recognised that the All Blacks were playing some excellent rugby. They were beginning to think, like us, that we could win it. Every which way you turned the World Cup jumped out at you. The TV had endless hours devoted to it, the papers continuously speculated about the 'correct' line-up and the possible outcome of the final, while the shops were doing good business in memorabilia.

David Kirk had become a media attraction, and he did a good job of deflecting some of the not-always-welcome attention away from the rest of the team. His fresh face, his fluid oratory and the fact that he was a doctor gave him an alluring appeal to PR men. His clean-cut image also did more than just improve the All Blacks South African-soiled image, he probably improved the image of rugby in New Zealand as a whole. Many parents must have watched him driving a steam-roller through the traditional perception of rough, uncouth rugby players and let their sons go out to play again.

As players we obviously saw the interest in ourselves rising along with that of the World Cup as a whole. The number of autograph hunters had been gradually increasing from the outset and was now reaching a crescendo. One of the items favoured by fans was the autographed rugby ball. From day one we had been happy to slap a monograph or two on a couple of balls, but by the time we returned to Auckland for the final we needed special signing sessions. About one hundred balls at a time were brought into our main coaching room in the hotel, and we had to sit down to sign each one then pass it on. We tried to keep it methodical by staying in alphabetical order to make sure that we didn't miss anybody out on any of the balls. To an outsider it must have looked as if we were running some sort of rugby ball embellishing factory. The sessions used to take nearly an hour and a half at a time, and we had to do one or two a week to satisfy the demand.

The expectations of what seemed like the whole of New Zealand weighed heavily on our shoulders. We hadn't wanted to let anybody down from the start of the tournament but to come this far and then fail would possibly have been worse. As a team we also had a score to settle with France regarding that second test defeat in Nantes. The taste of losing had been bitter and it was still extremely fresh in all of our memories. The disappointment and frustration of not being able to do anything about it until now had been very real. It was going to be one game that we simply had to win or we would never be able to hold our heads up high again.

On the big day we went through our normal routines and then watched the build-up on the TV. It was quite odd seeing and listening to the media preparing for something that we were going to do. Here we were in the hotel seeing everybody waiting for us to arrive, and we hadn't even started to leave yet. By the time we went down for our last team meeting there were a reported ten thousand spectators in the stadium, more than two hours before kick-off.

The sight of all those people arriving started me off on the negative thoughts and doubts that were becoming standard for me before a major game;

Had I bitten off more than I could chew ?

Was I up to it ?

Was I going to let everybody down by playing badly ?

Should I even be with the team at all ?

Can I play as well as I did last time ?

Was last time a fluke ?

Am I really good enough ?

This time my misgivings seemed to realise just how important the game was going to be and I almost felt sick. One of the stranger feelings that I, and a number of the other players felt, was that of being alone. The pressures and expectations appeared to be coming from everybody and every quarter, giving me a sense of isolation in my cause.

What was said at that final team meeting isn't in my memory. I must have been just too nervous. BJ will have said something, as would Kirky, probably about concentrating on the job in hand and not getting soaked up by the atmosphere. My subconscious picked up phrases which included terms like "be precise", "get clinical" and "don't choke" but I haven't a clue what went with them.

We were already in our smart blazers and our kit bags were packed, so we went straight out to the waiting buses. As we emerged from the foyer we were met by cheers and rapturous applause. About two hundred people had turned out to give us a buoyant sending off. This time nobody raced towards us to get an autograph and nobody wanted an interview, because they knew that we were concentrating intensely on the coming game. That unselfish behaviour and the fact that they had turned out to see us for just a few minutes made me finally realise that neither I, nor any of the team, were really alone. They were behind us and they genuinely wanted us to win.

As the bus pulled out of the car park I looked at everybody waving and I thought what a difference six months had made. I remembered being confronted by those anti-apartheid protestors on our way out to tour France and their less than friendly chants. I recollected the Labour government's opposition to the Cavaliers' tour of South Africa and the bad-mouthing that they'd dished out. The same government now viewed the All Blacks as one of New Zealand's best exportable commodities and they heaped praise on us in match programmes.

The journey took about half-an-hour from the hotel on the North Shore to the stadium on the South. At every set of red traffic lights we were given encouragement by passers-by. Most of them were on their way home to watch the game, going to a pub to watch the game or going somewhere else to watch the game. It did indeed feel as if we had the backing of the whole nation. The level of interest had to be seen to be believed. As most Americans can remember where they were when J.F.Kennedy was assassinated; most New Zealanders can remember where they were when they watched the World Cup final.

Yet more people greeted us when we got off the bus and we were applauded all the way down the long corridors into the spartan changing rooms. We took a few minutes in there savouring the peace and quiet then went out to 'inspect' the pitch. Yes, it was still there. And so was the expectant crowd, by then up to about twenty thousand.

Back in the changing rooms I put on my sacrosanct jersey and yet again my doubts evaporated like rain drops on a hot tin roof. I had acquired my Captain Scarlet-like invincibility and I could focus on what I had to do. Religiously, I mouthed my various jobs to myself; taking the high ball, finding touch, making tackles and joining the back-line as often as possible.

Kirky and Buck both gave us very emotional speeches, which gave me a tingle down the back of my spine. "Remember Nantes" was the shout and we streamed out onto the pitch to line-up for the national anthems. The stands were packed to their brim with forty-six thousand screaming fans. All of our ears rang with the din. If anybody was shouting for France they were totally drowned out. The only thing I managed to hear above the noise was Serge Blanco, who put his hand on my shoulder and said, "Good luck".

The Marseillaise came first and it was treated with the respect that you would expect from a rugby crowd but not from a soccer crowd.

Then came the New Zealand anthem, God of Nations, sung by the Auckland Rugby Union executive 'rock singer' Lew Pryme, and I had to concentrate on remembering the words, "God defend New Zealand...". It's not that I'd forgotten them or didn't know them, just that they had been pushed to the back of my mind by everything else. Modern TV camera lenses make it imperative that you do at least mumble the anthem, or else everyone watching will think that you don't care. Patriotism and Nationalism are two words that I don't normally like, but everybody singing along gave, even me, an outsider, a feeling of pride. I had never heard a New Zealand crowd sing the national anthem with any gusto before.

We started the game with a hiss and a roar. Almost before the French knew the kick-off had been taken we were in the lead. Murray Pierce had started on a high which he was to maintain all game. The opposition couldn't touch him in the line-outs and they were forced into an early infringement. Kirky got the ball, almost casually walked back to the twenty-two and tapped it to Foxy from the right-hand touchline. All the hours kicking practice that he'd put in, with me catching and returning his balls, paid off. A simple easing back of his leg, on his wrong side, sent the ball slotting between the posts for a drop-goal, 3-0.

A couple of minutes later Kirky put a high ball up, just to the left side of the pitch, which we challenged for. The ball came our way, and from the ruck it was quickly fired out to Bullet. I saw a gap outside his shoulder and took the ball off him. As I clutched it in, I felt Philippe Sella bearing down on me so I passed it to Greeno who was running up on my left.

At that point I realised I should loop round and look for a gap in case their winger got sucked in to tackle Greeno. This I did, and it appeared to be working perfectly with a breach materialising in the defence to give me a clear view of the try-line. Sadly the pass to me was a couple of inches off target and I saw it floating gently above my head. I had to make an instant choice and I let it go into touch. If I had gone for it, the prospect was that I would have knocked forward. My first chance had gone begging.

We won the ensuing French line-out and Foxy took another crack at a drop-goal. This time, however, Franck Mesnel charged it down to send the ball spinning across the front of the gapping goalmouth. Patrice Lagisquet was first there, only to look up and see AJ about to plough into him. Again the ball was sent pirouetting to the ground and Jonesy retrieved it.

By now I had joined Bullet on the right wing and we looked expectantly towards Jonesy for the pass. The try-line was again beckoning and either one of us was going to have an easy score. As we screamed at him, we both saw Jonesy twist inside and go for the line himself. I threw my arms up in despair and started to moan, "Oh no !". However, I'd just got to the "Oh" when I saw him reach out and place the ball down to push the score out to 9-0. Not to look a fool, I changed my despair into celebration saying, "Oh... great try" and throwing my arms up in jubilation. My second chance had gone begging.

Gallic pride was now at stake and their desire not to let anybody down must have been as strong as ours. Despite being over-run by Jonesy, Buck and AJ, the French stepped up their own game and came back at us. Eric Champ and Laurent Rodriguez started playing our forwards at their own game with a lot of swift running from scrums and rucks. Their back line containing that maestro Serge Blanco, with his counterparts Sella and Lagisquet, also starting to look as dangerous as rats trapped in a corner.

As the ball began to be jigged from right to left, and back again, it was our turn to tackle. Steve McDowell and Gary Whetton came in to their own and acted like a brick wall with steel reinforcements. Jonesy also showed that he was as good in defence as he was in attack with a telling challenge on Sella in full flight. When they did break down, of course, I was there to lend a hand. Between us, we all soaked up everything that they could throw at us before the interval to leave the score at 9-0.

That second part of the first half served notice that we had a fight on our hands. With the wind behind our backs in the first half we had wanted to be points up by the break. Disturbingly, their counter attacks had limited our tally and, with the rain starting to fall, we were worried that it wasn't going to be enough.

As if to prove the point, Didier Camberabero sailed an enormous penalty over the posts from the left flank to put the French back in it at 9-3. Fortunately this proved to be their high point. The opposition having the cheek to score served to kick-start our forwards, who once again motored and drove at the French weaknesses. Having thrown their all at us, they could not respond.

Foxy put over a couple of penalties which gave us a bit of a buffer and signalled the start of our purple patch. Fifteen metres out from the French goal line, Jonesy sprang up to tap the ball down to Kirky, who threw the ball open to Tails. He worked a scissors with Bullet in mid-field to set the ball up for our loose-forwards. Foxy ran blind from there, taking the ball with him on a half-break and fed to Jonesy who, one-handedly, tossed Kirky the final pass for him to score, 19-3.

When Foxy made his half-break, I had come on his outside looking for another gap. It had appeared and I'd shouted as loud as I could. Whether he heard me or not didn't matter because his turn back inside proved to be the right option. Nevertheless, my third chance had gone begging.

Unsatisfied, Kirky took-off again from the re-start like a cat being chased by a dog. His run only came to an end under the weight of three defenders, and he set the ball up for our loose-forwards. In one beautiful movement, Buck took it up and smashed his way through another couple of metres before dumping it on JK. From there it was down to speed. JK, who has sometimes been criticised for his lack of outright speed, showed a clean pair of heels to everyone, despite having hamstring trouble which was to put him out of action for several months to come. This time I was no where near and couldn't claim another chance gone begging.

Foxy's inevitable boot gave us another six points and at 29-3 we knew that it was in the bag. Maybe we relaxed a little and that may have been the reason for Pierre Berbizier getting France's consolation try in the dying minutes to make it 29-7. As Camberabero scored the conversion, Kirky called us all over into a huddle. I thought that he was going give us a roasting for not keeping a clean sheet because, after all, we were still 'remembering Nantes'. Instead, as I pushed my way between the sodden shirts of the forwards, I heard him say, "Well done boys, we've won the World Cup !". And with that, the final whistle blew.

Chapter 11

Celebration and Sobriety

Time for celebration had arrived, but first I dedicated a few seconds to personal solemnity and inner reflection. I'd done more than my own fair share of worrying since leaving Lewisham in 1984. Many times I'd lain awake wondering if I was going to let people down, including myself, by failing. Winning the World Cup was like having a massive weight lifted off my shoulders. I'd done my job well and proven myself. Those thoughts were only broken by a couple of friends from Wellington who had run onto the pitch contrary to instructions. They slapped me on the back and bellowed, "Well done, Kipper".

My first reaction was to grin, then, mindful of the All Blacks dour image, I broke into a liberal smile. Elsewhere, others were hugging one another and commiserating with the French. Above the stadium there was a magnificent rainbow.

As if drawn by some sort of magnet the team started to congregate at the entrance of the stairs up to the presentation rostrum. It took some moments for us all to get there as we shook hands with everybody in sight and slowly pushed our way through the milling throng who'd taken over the pitch. Inside silence reigned, apart from the rhythmic clatter of our studs on the concrete floor. As we climbed the steps, each of us returned to our own thoughts. Then, at the top, we burst out onto the platform and the applause of those standing around.

The din was tremendous. Behind the loudest explosions of those clapping to our left and right you could sense the whole audience appreciating our achievement. I could hear a few voices above the racket saying "Well done", and other such minor statements, which didn't stand a chance of matching the emotions I was feeling. Kirky lifted The Cup and the noise level rose to a new high. As if in self-protection my senses started to dim, the onlookers receded and events became a bit of a blur. I remember picking up my winners medal from Albert Ferrasse, and walking down the other side with the pandemonium still to either side, but that's about all.

One thing I do regret, looking back on those triumphant moments, was the fact that we never took a lap of honour. Situations like that only come around once in a lifetime, and I think we should have savoured it as much as possible. Apart from revelling in our own glory, there were spectators all round the pitch who would have liked to have seen The Cup at closer quarters. A quick run around would have given them a chance to provide us with their own special cheer, and would have made them feel a bit more as if they were part of the celebrations. I know the New Zealander's way is not to show off but considering the support we'd had, I don't think one lap would have gone down too badly.

The atmosphere back in the changing rooms was subdued. Everybody had a smile on their face and there was a lot of hugging going on, but I don't think anybody had the energy to do anything else. Also, supplementary to our tiredness, was the fact that none of us really knew what to do. And the question still stands in my head to this day - what, exactly, are you supposed to do when you have just won the World Cup ?

While we were in the process of coming to terms with our victory and getting changed, there was a first as far as anybody in the team knew; a TV crew were allowed into the changing rooms. To satisfy their quest for merriment we obliged by doing the Haka.

Once changed, I went upstairs to the after-match function and spotted Dad. The expression on his face told me everything. He was obviously sharing the same emotions as I was. It was nice to know that he could participate in such an important moment in my life. He had his camera with him and took a full roll of pictures. Sadly, though, the developers managed to destroy the film before they made any prints, so we were left without a permanent reminder of the day.

The function included an enormous and delicious meal, enjoyed by the teams from all the countries who'd taken part in the competition, seated on separate tables. We were very aware that everybody in the room apart from ourselves were basically losers, and we didn't want to rub their noses in our success. So we stayed very sober and lived up to our sullen image. Under the surface, we had overcome our inward reflections and were itching to let loose with our revelry. All we wanted to do was jump about, wave our arms and shout, but the blazers, collars and ties restricted us like straight-jackets. Also holding us in our seats was a seemingly endless procession of boring dialogues from the top table, just like headmasters' at Speech Day. It was a classic case of the hierarchy trying to impress everyone but falling well short of the mark. An address to four-hundred tired rugby players should have concentrated on humour not doctrine.

Once we were set free, we got out of there as quickly as possible. Away from any controls, and the eye of the media, we got down to some pretty serious partying. At 4 a.m. I found myself behind the hotel reception throwing keys at anybody who came through the door. I don't know how I'd got there but I was wet from a dip in the swimming pool. At 5 a.m., I finally called an end to a brilliant and unforgettable day.

The next one, Sunday, started with a banging in my head and a taste in my mouth like the bottom of a budgie's cage. At 6:30 a.m., Zinny and Bernie McCahill were running around the hotel doing very loud and obviously effective impressions of cockerels. From the accents I couldn't tell if they were pretending to be French or not.

Another party had been arranged, this one with the theme of 'Golden Oldies'. A lot of past All Blacks from various generations turned up to have their feet set in concrete, like the film-stars do on Hollywood Boulevard. It wasn't the most dynamic of events that I've ever been part of, and there seemed to be an awful lot of standing around. Compared to the exhaustion and exuberance of the day before, it fell totally flat. The combination of faces from the past and boredom made it feel as if we hadn't just won the first ever World Cup. Those around us were more interested in watching concrete dry than celebrating our victory. I would rather have continued the raucous party of the night before with my team-mates.

We had all become very close during the campaign, which had lasted six weeks. Even though there were a lot of different personalities in the camp, we had all got on famously. There hadn't been any splits and everybody had supported one another to the full.

The loss of that intimacy, and the nadir of the 'day after', made our individual departures from the team hotel all the more sorrowful.

Withdrawal symptoms persisted upon my return to work on the Monday. A greater anti-climax is hard to imagine. One day I'm playing in the biggest game of my rugby career, trotting up to receive my World Cup winners-medal, and then two days later I'm reporting for work at a Wellington police station. All I wanted to do was wind back time and re-live those moments of exultation on the pitch again and again. It was very similar to the feeling you get when you return home after a fantastic holiday; I wanted the excitement to continue rather than having to revert to a 'normal' repetitious life. My Chief Inspector helped keep the memories alive, in a way, by putting me out on the beat with Murray Pierce. He thought that it would be good PR for the police if we were seen on the streets talking to children and passers-by. I suppose it was possibly post-climactic depression but my first cynical thoughts were that we were being used. The police were going to get a lot of publicity and someone, somewhere, was going to get a pat on the back for thinking about it.

Another indicator of the come-down I was experiencing, was the fact that a week after the final I played a game for Ories. Even though I always enjoyed playing for my club, it just wasn't the same. One week playing for the World Champions, next week playing for a mid-table Swindale Shield club side. It certainly served to cut me back down to size.

Adding to my melancholy were the sour-grapes coming from the media and the 'Home' Unions:

The European press, and the English in particular, gave us a bit of stick for the way the final had been played. In light of the universally acclaimed semi-final between Australia and France, they thought we had played a tedious match. That attitude showed no concept of how to win at all. The conditions hadn't allowed us to throw the ball out wide, and with speed merchants such as Sella, Lagisquet and Blanco in the opposition, waiting to pounce on dropped passes, who can blame us. Just look at what happened to Australia when they tried it. Exhibition games against Barbarian teams and Sevens tournaments are the places to take risks for the sake of being flashy, not tests. Test matches are about victory, to prove that you can outscore the opposition. And if there was ever a test that had to be won, then it was that inaugural World Cup final. If we had only needed to score one point, and then defend for seventy-nine minutes to win, we would have done it.

Also starting to emerge were backside-covering allegations from the British Unions, that the All Blacks were receiving under-the-table payments for playing. In essence they were looking for an excuse to hide their own poor showings in The Cup. If England, Scotland, Ireland and Wales had done better then we would have heard nothing about it. Instead, they tried to make out that we were professionals and that's why we were so good. They couldn't accept that their staid old-school-tie system wasn't working.

Their claims centred around three advertisements that were shown extensively on New Zealand TV during The Cup. The first one was for our main sponsor, Steinlager, which showed us in a simulated changing -room situation and then on the pitch. The filming had taken nearly two days to complete and I had been on night-shift at the time. As a result I turned up dog-tired and tried to sneak off for quick sleeps between 'takes'. The first sequence showed us preparing for a game. I was in the background psyching myself up by banging my head on one of the lockers. Others were running on the spot or putting their gum shields in. The next sequence showed us 'during' a game. I had loads of make-up plastered on my face along with brown boot-polish to act as mud and a few sprigs of grass sticking out of my ears. To make us look tired, they sprayed us all with cold water from a nearby hosepipe. The whole experience was one that I would not choose to do off my own bat. Of course we were paid expenses for attending the studios and making the advert. My total payment, for both days work when I should have been sleeping, amounted to NZ$150 or about £50, which had to cover all my travel and food, etc. If that is equatable to being a professional player, then I'd rather be a policeman.

The second advert which prompted 'professionalism' allegations included Frano and Buck throwing cans of paint around while dressed in their rugby jerseys. The third showed Andy Dalton, who was, in fact, a farmer at the time, driving a tractor and promoting a particular brand. Non-expense money from all of these ads went either directly to the New Zealand Union or to the players own clubs, such as North Harbour for Frano and Buck's.

The latter two advertisements had needed to be scrapped in the middle of the tournament, because of complaints from other teams, just before our quarter-final. The night before the game, Bob Stuart, councillor at the New Zealand Rugby Union and member of the International Rugby Board, came down and explained that there had been a couple of complaints about the ads. The two teams, who we were lead to believe were Scotland and Italy, both wanted New Zealand to be kicked out of the World Cup ! Naturally pretty swift moves were made to appease these complaints, however unjust. Both the paint and the tractor adverts were removed from the TV and we were allowed to continue playing. The Steinlager ad was allowed to continue.

In case the same threats were going to raise their ugly heads after the Scotland game, one ex-player decided on a few steps of self-protection. He quickly assembled a collection of signed affidavits by past players from the Home Unions. Each one stated that they had been paid cash for playing rugby in Britain and various other European countries including Italy. If there had been another attempt to have us expelled then those statements would have been waived in several faces.

The complaints were totally ridiculous, hypocritical and smacked of unbridled envy. I was an integral part of the All Blacks during the World Cup and then for a couple of years after that. In all that time I can categorically say that I was NEVER paid cash to play rugby. The first hard currency I ever saw, from all the work that I'd put in over the years, came from Leeds Rugby League Football Club when I signed for them in 1990.

One good aspect about the Home Unions making those childish excuses for their own failures, was that they brought the subject of payments for playing Rugby Union into the open; where does amateurism end and professionalism start ? For many years, top players from all around the world had been, and still are being, paid indirectly for going out onto the pitch. The usual way of bending the amateur rules was by paying a player for a non-existent job. Lots of clubs 'import' foreign players, or poach the best domestic players, with offers of work that they don't have to do. Provided they turn out for the club every week, they can pick up their manilla envelope without having to do anything else. The same player will often get a club car, club house, club food allowance, club clothing allowance, etc, etc. If that isn't professionalism, what is ?

In my opinion, even school-children and students can be classified as professionals. Many a promising child has been given a scholarship to go to a top rugby-playing public school just because of his abilities on the field. By remaining good at rugby his next step is a place at Oxford or Cambridge to study Land Economy or some other superfluous subject. From there the money markets beckon, or a job in a large company run by an old-school-tie director who is fond of rugby.

So why, therefore, are there so many accusations between Unions about professionalism ? None of them are exactly squeaky clean. And why is there so much fuss made when somebody such as myself turns openly professional ? The only real difference between a Rugby League pro and a Rugby Union pro is that one is paid in cash, and therefore pays tax, while the other is paid in kind.

One of the biggest ironies, to me, is that there's more money to be made in Rugby Union than Rugby League. In League it is only the top echelons of players who can afford to be without another job. The bulk of club players receive a relatively small amount for their labour. In Union, on the other hand, comparable small fry can make a good living at the game. Admittedly their payments are unlikely to be in cash, but they will be well looked after by their clubs. A glance at a club's accounts is unlikely to show anything out of the ordinary, but if you start asking detailed questions you will probably find a scarcity of information in some quarters.

An even bigger paradox, to my way of thinking, are all those people who made the complaints against us during and after the World Cup. They were fine, standing up there on their high-horses, but how much were they being paid to spout about keeping the game amateur ?

Chapter 12

Travelling the World

As the World Cup euphoria was winding down and we were regaining the Bledisloe Cup from Australia with a 30-16 win in Sydney, Japan asked if the All Blacks could tour their country. There was a lot of debate but eventually the visit was agreed, and a squad was assembled after the New Zealand National Championships to fly out to Tokyo. Various pundits said that it was going to be a waste of time making the trip because the Japanese weren't a strong enough rugby nation to give us any real opposition. This is perhaps true, but how can any nation improve unless they play against stronger sides ? The fact many people failed to understand was that a Japanese telecommunications company, KDD, had stepped in at the last moment and virtually saved the World Cup from financial disaster. The very least New Zealand could do as the hosts of the World Cup (since it is they who would have suffered the embarrassment if it had failed) was to agree to the request.

Brian Lochore had retired after the World Cup so the Union had appointed the other two selectors, John Hart and Grizz Wyllie, to take over. They decided to 'blood' a couple of new players, including Schuey, and appointed Buck as the new captain. I was chosen as the only full-back, and it was indicated that I'd be used as a work-horse, playing in all five of the scheduled games including the two unofficial 'test' matches.

We were totally blinded when we walked through customs and set foot on Japanese soil. It seemed as if the whole world had turned up for our arrival with flash-cameras. Looking straight ahead I was stunned by the brilliance of the small explosions, and they caused me to turn my head away. I then found myself looking at a new set of fans who immediately let loose with their salvo of illumination.

When I managed to get my sunglasses on, and my eyes had acclimatised to the incoming rays, I noticed that most people were wearing fake All Black shirts. At first I was surprised, because I'd always thought there was a worldwide copyright on the Silver Fern. Then, I began to think of the implications. If we hadn't been world champions, they probably wouldn't have been wearing the shirts. It was doubtful the New Zealand Union was ever going to see revenue from the sales, and we players certainly weren't. Therefore, I concluded that somebody, somewhere, was making money out of our fame, which had been brought about by our own hard work. That struck me as being totally unfair.

As a player I couldn't profit from my rugby, other than in kind. Occasionally I was doing some promotional work, but the money was going directly to the Union, my club or the police. I didn't begrudge those three parties from profiting, because they had all given me plenty of help in the past with my training and playing. However, I did begrudge people whom I hadn't even met benefiting at my expense. It seemed to me as if everybody, apart from myself, was making money from my rugby exploits.

Our first game was in Tokyo against the home 'B' side calling themselves 'Japan Selection' and we won 94-0. I scored three tries and Schuey made his debut. We then had four days before our next game which was to be the first unofficial test in Osaka. A quick ride on the Bullet-Train and a short bus ride took us to our 'hotel' which was actually a Buddhist Temple at Tenre. Everywhere we went we had to wear something different on our feet. Outdoor shoes had to be left at the entrance where we were given our 'inside' pair of thongs. They could be worn around the temple but we needed another pair for use in our bedrooms. There were also 'specialist' pairs for going into the dining room, the toilet and the washroom.

For a pleasant change we were each given our own room. As could be expected they were also traditionally Japanese; very small, clean and spartan with several cushions on the floor, a central table and crockery for making tea. One concession to 'modern' life was a vacuum flask which contained hot water for making the brew.

I never saw anybody enter my room and there wasn't anybody around who looked like chamber maids. However, the flask was always topped up, as if by a ghost, every time I turned my back. There was also another presence who uncannily knew when I wanted to go to bed. I'd return to find my cushions spirited away with a futon put in their place and the covers invitingly pulled back.

Putting us in there was a great idea and I think everybody enjoyed it. It would have been too easy to just put us into Western style hotels and have done with it. This way we got to see something of Japanese life rather than simply Western life with unreadable characters on the front. As a retreat it also served to keep the media away from us as they were hounding our every footstep.

Training took place at local university grounds and, as was customary, the team was announced at one of the sessions. Frano Botica was picked, which meant that Foxy wouldn't be playing. As a result I was given the kicking duties. Naturally I was delighted that Harty and Grizz showed enough faith to give me the extra responsibility. It made me feel good about myself. But, it also caused my usual self-doubts to rise up again.

John, the dedicated person he is, always exposed himself to a build up of tension before a game whether it be club football or a test match. This was clearly evident in one game when he arrived at the ground and he had forgotten his playing gear at the hotel. He also used to partake in a special ritual of drinking four raw eggs with milk on a match day thinking it was good for him, until he was told otherwise. This was a real delight for John because the taste had never appealed to him.
JOHN SCHUSTER

The day before the game we were taken to see the ground where we were due to play, but we couldn't find it. All we discovered was a golf driving range. This didn't strike us as unusual, because we knew the Japanese were crazy about their golf as well as rugby. A few enquiries were made and it slowly dawned on us, the driving range was the pitch, or rather the pitch had been used as a driving range. It looked as if there had been a terrible hail shower, there were balls everywhere. Nevertheless, as is the way in Japan, when we turned up for the match, all the golf balls had been cleared away, the divots had been replaced and it looked as if the ground had never been used before.

Similarly, part way into the match it was looking as if I'd never kicked goals before. My attempts were going wayward and I was getting extremely worried. Only one of my kicks had scored from four efforts. With the amount of tries we were likely to score, that was going to mean an embarrassing number of misses. Fortunately, things started to go my way after that initial hiccup, and I got the next eleven straight over.

Although we were physically a lot bigger than the Japanese they caused us a lot of problems, particularly in the first half. They were very committed to giving us a good game and they didn't concede an inch without a fight. Their tackling was distinctive and fairly effective. It consisted of a kamikaze-like headlong dive into our legs. Before long we were all hobbling around with ever deepening purple bruises on our shins. Each time I got the ball I would make a few metres and then, tssschung, the oriental missiles would find their target.

The half-time score was only 20-0 which showed their dedication. In the second half, we did better as the home side began to tire (perhaps their heads were becoming as battered as our shins). The final score was 74-0 and I managed to add a try to my ten conversions and two penalties. My personal tally was, therefore, a total of 30 points which equalled the existing world test record. Unfortunately for me, it didn't count because the test was unofficial, i.e. played against a non-International Rugby Board member country. Oddly enough, if I'd scored as many against Japan in the World Cup, only months earlier, it would have counted.

My third game in a row came only three days later. We beat an Asian Barbarians side, drawn from Japan, Hong Kong, Tiawan and Korea, by 96-3 and I scored two tries. The opposition were captained by Englishman Nigel Pearson, from Hong Kong, who said that he found it difficult leading a side of which only one third understood what he was saying. He needn't have offered any excuses because his side played well, despite the final score, and forced us into many errors.

Harty, a died-in-the-wool perfectionist, got us all together after the game and expressed his dissatisfaction at our performance. Accepting our points tally, he pointed to the number of knock-ons, dropped passes and penalties that we had given away. No player was above the rebuke and we were all told how many errors we had made as individuals. In front of the whole team, a typical analysis would go like this:

"Well, Kipper, how do you think you played ?"

"Not too bad"

"I think you had a shocker. How many errors did you make ?"

"About two or three"

"Actually you made five. If everybody made five then that would be seventy-five errors and you would lose to any of the Home Unions or Australia".

If you felt like taking him to task on your number of errors, then you were in for a hard time because he had made a list of each one. It detailed where you had been on the pitch, what you had been trying to do and who was near you. It served to put everybody on the same level. Those who thought they had played a blinder were brought down to earth, whilst those who thought they had played appallingly were told they hadn't done too badly. Overall, I think it was great for team motivation, one way or another.

That roasting after the Barbarians game got us really fired up for the second unofficial test just another four days later. As a result we ran out winners by a massive 106-4, scoring nineteen tries. Thirteen of those tries went to the forwards with Zinny picking up four of them. I didn't touch-down and, with Foxy back in the team, I didn't get on the scoresheet at all. Buck didn't allow us to relax for one moment during the whole game. He kept driving us onwards and was constantly pushing us to keep amassing the points. When the Japanese scored their try after half-time, Buck got us in a huddle and snarled in no uncertain terms that we mustn't let in another. We didn't dare.

Harty's analysis afterwards indicated that we had made an unheard of low number of errors - only four in the whole eighty minutes. It was the first time that Japan had conceded a century and only the second time that the All Blacks had scored one (the first being against South Australia in 1974). When we scored the points which took us over the ton, the thirty-eight thousand crowd all stood and applauded us. Although they were seeing their side annihilated, they could appreciate that they were also seeing some top-class rugby being played. Anywhere else there would have been total silence and one or two players would have been strung up afterwards.

The last game, three days after the second 'test' making my aggregate five games in fourteen days, was against a Japanese President's World XV. The opposition team included players such as John Jeffrey, Gavin Hastings and Dean Richards. We knew that it was going to be a different game from the rest, and that we were going to experience some shuddering first-time tackles for a change.

The weather was also different and consisted of unrelenting rain. The pitch turned into a quagmire and the ball seemed as slippery as a bar of soap in the after-match bath. The combination of a larger opposition and poorer conditions served to limit our try scoring to six, giving us a win by 38-9.

Although devastated by the size of their second-test defeat, the Japanese team joined us in a drinking session afterwards. They were a great bunch of lads and seemed to really love their rugby. As a favour they took some of us around one or two of the less-well-known bars in Tokyo. After that they wanted to take us night-clubbing. I politely declined feeling the worse for wear and left Schuey, my room-mate, with some of the others to paint the town red.

Next morning I was woken by the telephone ringing in our room. It was Schuey. I wasn't surprised because I knew it was his turn to be 'Duty Boy' which entailed helping the manager get everybody up, pack all the gear into the coach and generally make sure our departure went smoothly. At the moment I recognised his voice, I also noticed the time, it was 10:15 a.m. and I knew we were supposed to be on the coach by 10:30 a.m. My eyes slowly focused and I noticed that Schuey's bed hadn't been slept in.

"Kipper, Kipper," he said.

"Schuey, you've let me over-sleep," I started.

"Shut-up Kipper and listen"

"Where are you ? Are you in reception ?"

"No. Shut-up, that's the problem"

"What are you talking about ?"

"I don't know where I am. What's the address of the hotel ?"

"Schuey. What the hell are you talking about ?". I was still coming out of my sleep and couldn't make sense of the situation.

"I'm lost - somewhere in Tokyo I think"

"But you're on duty today"

"I know, but I went clubbing with the Japanese lads and ended up sleeping on one of their floors. The silly bugger's gone off to work and I haven't got a clue where I am. I'll have to get a taxi back to the hotel. Now tell me the address and be quick about it." He sounded a bit agitated.

I contemplated giving him the wrong address but thought better of it (or thought more about his potential retribution) and read the correct one out from the telephone pad. Within minutes of putting the receiver down, I was up, dressed and had packed both our bags. I stumbled all the way down to reception with both arms full, only to find that I wasn't on my own in getting up late. With Schuey not dishing out the wake-up calls, almost everybody was behind schedule.

We climbed onto the waiting coach and took a head count. One missing - Schuey. For twenty minutes we sat there with the engine running and the manager standing just outside the door tapping his watch. Suddenly a yellow taxi screeched into view and Schuey jumped out. Climbing onto the coach he was greeted by a wall of jeers and abuse.

"Where's our lager ?"; "Yeh, and where's our meat ?"; shouted two voices from the back. Schuey's eyes widened and his face went ashen. He did a quick about turn, jumped off and ran into the hotel. We had been given loads of beer by Steinlager to see us through the tour. And the New Zealand Meat Marketing Board, for whom we had done a couple of evening PR jobs, had given us a pile of meat for a barbecue later on that day. The room where everything had been left was searched, but there was no sign of it. The Japanese ghosts had cleaned it all away, and it was probably waiting to be picked up in another room. Unfortunately the management didn't know where it was either, and there was no time to look for it. Schuey returned to the coach with his head down and duly received even more abuse. If it had been a school trip he would have been made to sit at the front with the teacher, naughty boy.

Although the best of mates, rooming with John on football trips was always a burden. Not only was he messy, untidy and forgetful, but you could never depend on him for the usual toiletries, for, like myself, he only packs a toothbrush and the bare minimum of clothing. An incident not to be forgotten was when rooming with John during preparation for an All Black trial. A meeting was scheduled for 10:00 a.m., the alarm did not go off and we both ended up sleeping in. Anyone who knows Alex Wyllie would know that he is heavy on discipline and does not condone lateness. Anyway, we got to the meeting clearly showing signs that we had just hopped out of bed. The boys were all in fits of laughter, but to our relief Wyllie tore strips off the person who had roomed us together.

JOHN SCHUSTER

Harty and Grizz were, in my mind at least, the two best available coaches in the country after the World Cup. It was only natural that they be asked to look after the squad during the tour to Japan. I had expected them to be equal partners, so it was a bit of a surprise when Harty was named as the 'senior' coach, albeit just for the tour. It was fairly obvious that they couldn't work 'under' one another so equality would have been the best thing.

More of a surprise was Harty's actions once the tour had been completed. He seemed to assume that he was going to stay the 'senior' coach/selector and he gave several press interviews pointing the way ahead for New Zealand rugby. I didn't know what was going on in Harty's mind but I thought that he would have had more intelligence than to come out with those sort of comments. Perhaps the media were stitching him up but it looked as if he was singing his own praises. Knowing the New Zealand Union (and the New Zealand public), he should have realised that they don't like self-acclamation.

Consequently I, for one, didn't think it was a bombshell when Grizz was subsequently appointed top man. If Harty had stayed quiet, I think he would have been given the job. As recompense, he was appointed as one of the sub-selectors, along with Earle Kirton. Then he saw fit to pull out, saying that if he couldn't have the number one position there was no way he could justify having so much time off work.

It was Grizz therefore, who was the main instigator of my selection for the All Blacks in 1988. I was conscious of the fact that I had been picked on the basis of my 1987 form, because I done nothing which would have warranted my selection in '88. Putting the Silver Ferned jersey on for the first time that year was more of a relief than anything else.

The opening game of our season was against Wales who were touring New Zealand and not having a very good time of it. We ran out winners by 52-3 and I had a good solid game, scoring one try, which pleased me immensely. The size of our win would have been surprising but for the fact that they had struggled against the provincial sides. They were, after all, the triple crown winners that year. I felt very sorry for a few of their players such as Jonathan Davies, John Devereux and David Young, who were without doubt world-class players. But the team was very badly prepared and didn't appear to have much direction.

The second test was two weeks later in Auckland and we won by another large margin, 54-9. It was a harder game but we improved our play correspondingly. There's no doubt that the Welsh were on a downward slope which had started in the World Cup, whereas we had improved on our 1987 form because we had managed to keep the same team together.

After their humiliating tour, several Welshmen re-opened the 'All Blacks are professional players' routine. Still they refused to accept that the system in Britain was wrong. They preferred to slag us off, rather than look inward to see what was the problem. No wonder so many of that touring team really did turn professional with various Rugby League clubs.

As the 1988 season progressed I became more and more aware of the profits that people were making out of my rugby playing. Even the police were at it, with me spending almost as much time making appearances at various police functions as on the beat.

In an attempt to set this right, I agreed to do a weekly column called 'The Last Line' for the Dominion newspaper. I was paid approximately NZ$100 per column and the first cheque came direct to my house, made payable to myself. By that stage I was beginning to think that I should keep the money, because I was having to work for it. I did, after all, have to put time aside to prepare the column. The agreement wasn't dependent on my actually playing rugby.

However, I was fully aware that there would be prying eyes watching me, probably looking to make another profit out of an 'exposé'. I returned the cheque to the newspaper, asked them to make it out to Ories and to send it directly to the club. To cover my backside, I also informed the National and Wellington Unions letting them know what was going on.

Some of my first columns were written on the '88 tour of Australia. We opened the trip with a series of wins; against Western Australia 60-3, Ranwick 25-9, Australia B 28-4 and New South Wales Country 29-4. Then we travelled to Sydney for the first of three tests.

The importance of getting a good start in the series forced the selectors to field a side similar to the one which won the World Cup. Schuey was one of the exceptions, and he was chosen to make his test debut because Tails had broken his hand against Australia B. I've never seen him so nervous as he was the day before the game. Wherever we were, we used to play the odd game of cricket in the corridors of the hotel in which we were staying. We only used a tennis ball, bowling was limited to under-arm and no shots were allowed above knee hight. However, Schuey's nerves showed themselves in a, luckily non-destructive, spate of over-arm full-tosses and wild hook-shots.

It was obvious that the sooner he got his first test out of the way, the better it would be for everybody's personal and mental safety. However, I couldn't really give him much advice on how to stay cool. Even though I was becoming an 'old hand', as far as test matches were concerned, I was still prone to an attack of nerves before I put on The Jersey.

In Australia, I was doing my usual routine of having a chat with players in their rooms before the team meeting. John was obviously feeling nervous about the game, was on the lavatory and was running late. The team eventually boarded the coach to go to the ground, but I could see that John was still very worried about something. It turned out he'd left his boots behind, and I had to send one of the reserves back to the hotel with the police to collect them.
ALEX WYLLIE

In the test we had a dream start and went 14-0 up within the first eleven minutes, and carried on to win by 32-7, which was the All Blacks' highest test score against the Wallabies in Australia. Going into the match, JK only needed two tries to pass Stu Wilson's try scoring record for the All Blacks which stood at nineteen. An early score put him level, and then I had the honour of creating the overlap for him to notch up his twentieth. A great moment for a great player at the age of only twenty-three. Another happy memory of that test was Schuey going in for his first test try. He had made a nervous start early on, but made no mistake when Joe Stanley and I sent him on his spectacular way to the line near the end.

Less happy was the reaction towards losing from the Aussie team, coach and media. First of all they complained that we had been overly aggressive and violent. Then they criticised the referee, Fred Howard from England, saying he was "abysmal" a "novice" and that he "wasn't up to the occasion". It's funny how the country that invented the phrase "Whingeing Pom" always seems to be leading the way.

Between the first and second tests, we played the Australian Capital Territory (winning 16-3), Queensland (27-12) and Queensland B (39-3). I played in all three, meaning that I'd been in all the games of the tour bar the Australia B game. It showed in my try tally and two against Queensland brought my aggregate up to five.

I was quite happy with my personal form, but as a squad we were becoming a bit tired and a bit jaded. We had played eight games, of which I'd played in seven, and we'd picked up a number of injuries. To cap it all we were made to face Australia in the second test only sixty-five hours after the end of the Queensland B game.

Thus, it wasn't completely surprising that we didn't repeat our big first-test win. The final score was a 19-19 draw, after we had buckled down to come back from a 16-6 deficit at half-time. Foxy actually had a chance to put us ahead in the last five minutes but missed a difficult kick. He was devastated. But that's how it often goes as a goal-kicker, glory or gloom.

To everybody in the team, it felt as though we had lost. You could have turned the clock back to Nantes in 1987 and the scenes would have been the same; long faces, drooping shoulders and heavy legs. From the dejection that was shown all evening and most of the next day, you wouldn't have believed that we had just retained the Bledisloe Cup by virtue of being the holders and not being defeated in the series.

That depression reached beyond the players and even got into the selectors veins. None of us knew how Grizz was going to take it. There were rumours that he was going to work us to the bone in training, and then there were counter-rumours that he was going to give us a day off. On our way to the next location it became evident which it was going to be. The bus pulled to a halt outside the Eastwood Rugby Club, and Grizz stood up "Right," he growled, "everybody off the bus, into the changing rooms and get changed, NOW !".

In the club there was a feeling of foreboding and lots of blame being thrown around; "It's all your fault", "No it's not", "I thought you said you heard Grizz say we were going to have a day off", "No I didn't, you did", etc. The only thing that stopped the bickering, was the smack of the door nearly coming off its hinges as Grizz burst in. "You all know what went wrong in Brisbane, don't you ?" he barked. Everybody stayed quiet and looked at the ground to avoid eye contact. "Spirit !," he said, "Now leave your jerseys on, and you've got forty five seconds to get into the bar !". Relief and smiles swept the room.

Once upstairs, the doors were closed and locked behind us. The bar shutters went up and the beer started to flow. Jonesy and those under the Doc were let off, but the rest of us knew what was expected of us. To start us off, Grizz made the squad stand in a huge circle, one behind the other, and told us to commence walking slowly. As we passed him and Jonesy at the bar we were handed a full pint and told to drink. By the time we had gone a full circle and returned to the bar, in about two minutes, we had to finish the pint and be ready to get another one. When we were all totally bloto, Grizz moved us on to another game, and then another, and then another...

It worked a treat. Although it is pretty hard to condone drinking and getting drunk for drinking's sake, this session had lots of spin-offs. In fact, I would go as far as to say, that's when the tour really started. Grizz had always been in charge of us based on rank, but from that moment on he was in charge with respect. We had learned that he did have a sense of humour and that he understood we weren't just rugby-playing machines. We also came together as a squad and started to relax in one another's company again. Smiles returned to our faces in training and the killer instinct sprang back into our veins.

And it showed in our results. We cruised through the next three games 45-9 against New South Wales B, 42-6 against New South Wales and 84-8 against a Victorian XV. In the second two of those games I scored six tries and, with Foxy getting injured, slotted over twelve conversions.

With the renewed spirit, there was no way that the Wallabies were going to match us in the final test. Just to make sure, Grizz gave us one of his 'growling' speeches. He sat us all down in the changing rooms about fifteen minutes before kick-off and laid into us. His first words were, "There's no such thing in rugby as Luck" and then he went on to tell us that we made our own 'luck'. For about five long minutes, he persisted in saying that we were going to get out of it what we put in and that we couldn't rely on 'luck' going our way. Eventually our heads bowed as he reached his crescendo and finished. There was silence as he looked around and said, "That's it, I've said my piece - Good Luck lads !". I had to bite the back of my hand to stop laughing.

With Grizz's words ringing in our ears, we went out and took the game to the Aussies, scoring a tasty 30-9 victory to round off the tour. Foxy returned from injury and picked up 18 points to take him over Don Clarke's record points aggregate in test matches of 207. I also got another touch-down which made me the highest try scorer of the tour with twelve, one ahead of JK on eleven and five ahead of Graeme Bachop on seven. A lot of the credit for my scores must go to Bullet who started to look for me as an option to the closely marked JK. However, I'd also learnt the lines that he and Terry Wright usually ran so I could anticipate the moves earlier and grab an extra metre on the defence that way. It's not often that anybody outscores the prolific JK, so I was fairly proud.

The lively mood in the team also had its effects off the pitch. While we were in Sydney we tried to see how many All Blacks would fit into the hotel lift. The answer was 'fifteen-but-the-lift won't-work-afterwards'. Of course we didn't know the second part of the answer when we pressed the buttons to go up to our rooms. Consequently we were all surprised when the cabin shuddered to a halt between floors.

With the exception of the new physio, David Abercrombie, I was the smallest in there and I was being squeezed from all sides. In fact, I felt more like a sardine than a kipper. As the temperature began to rise, the big boys started to get fidgety and I received more than one elbow in the face. Then they put their muscle to some good use and forced the lift doors open a few inches to let some air in. As the doors opened we could hear Alan Whetton, who had prised open the doors into the shaft above us with a broom handle, singing "Now is the hour for me to say goodbye...".

Being one of the new style lifts, there were strip lights in the roof and no exit hatch for us to climb out. So, basically, we were stuck, and there was nothing we could do. It was stiflingly hot and everybody was under threat of death if they should drop a smelly one. Eventually, fifty two minutes later, the hotel contacted the lift manufacturers and a technician came out to free us. By the time I was spat out onto the corridor floor, I had lost about five pounds in weight.

The Great Britain Rugby League team had played a President's XIII near Canberra the day before our game against the Australian Capital Territory. They had continued on to Brisbane for the next match in their tour and we had followed them, ending up in the same posh hotel. While we were there, JK and I found ourselves taking the same lift as Ellery Hanley and Phil Ford up to our rooms. We had a bit of a chat and wished one another luck in our mutual battles against the Aussies.

Back in my room I lay on my neatly made-up bed, and stared at the whitewashed ceiling instead of switching on the TV. The All Black Rugby Union and the Great Britain Rugby League squads were both touring Australia, both getting the same media coverage and both heaving their guts up while training as hard as possible. Yet they were getting paid for their efforts and we weren't, even though we were probably getting as large, if not larger, crowds. Something wasn't right, somewhere.

Most of us kept track of the Lions after that, and we all sat down to watch their final test against the Kangaroos. There was a huge cheer and a lot of admiration for Phil Ford when he threw about five side-steps one after the other to score a fantastic try. Little did I know that just three years later I'd be playing alongside him at Leeds.

Arriving back at Auckland airport there were a lot of people to meet us. It wasn't just the usual wives or girlfriends but parents, grandparents and friends had turned up along with a large contingent of general well-wishers.

Obviously I didn't have any family there, so I was happy when a little four year-old boy stepped forward with his mother. His name was David Greene and he had compiled a scrap book of the tour with a special emphasis on my exploits. As he handed it over to me he had a look of pride on his face. It was a very touching moment and one that I will never forget. I wanted to give him something in return so I shuffled around in my kit bag. Unfortunately, all I could find was an old pair of smelly All Black socks that I'd worn the day before in the test, but he took them nonetheless (I didn't look to see if his mother was holding her nose). Perhaps I didn't receive any money for the tour, but that little boy made up for it.

Chapter 13

No Rest for the Wicked

There wasn't even a rest upon returning from Australia. Next thing I knew, I was on Wellington's tour of the North Island. It all seemed like non-stop rugby and I felt myself going a bit stale. When we finally entered the closed season, I realised I was going to need a new challenge or my playing standard was going to suffer.

In the pub one Friday night, whilst contemplating what I could aim for, a bloke wandered over and started chatting about rugby. I'd grown used to it by this stage; although I'd never minded people coming to me and asking for an autograph, I normally objected when they pulled up a seat and interrupted my evening. However, on this occasion I let it go, and it proved to be a good move.

His name was Paul Hendry, and he went through the usual chit-chat about how I was playing, then started talking about advertising. Explaining that he had quite a lot of experience in the industry, he asked if I had ever thought about marketing myself. I said that I had, and that I thought we should talk about it at another time because we had both had a few beers.

A day or so later Paul rang me up and we arranged to meet over lunch. He quizzed me about what I was doing, particularly about promotional work for the police and said that it proved I was a marketable commodity. I knew at the time how much I was in demand for radio interviews, after-dinner speeches and guest appearances and I knew that JK had just started his own 'promotional' company, so I was very interested. The conversation went on, and we tried to figure out how it could be done whilst still preserving the 'amateur' status which was demanded of me by Union rules.

In the end we consulted with Pat Brunton, whom Paul had introduced to me as another person with working knowledge about individual promotion. And we all went along, with a lawyer, for discussions with the New Zealand Union. Surprisingly we were given a good reception and the Union were more helpful than obstructive. By the end of the meeting, we ascertained that the only way I could proceed was if I started a company and that it became my only full-time bona-fide occupation.

That posed a problem for me because no matter how much I wanted to redress the balance of others profiteering from my rugby, I couldn't leave my career in the police just in case the new venture failed. After all, I had just bought a house and I had a mortgage to pay.

An offer made to me a few months earlier by a friend called Eddie Wong-she sprang into my mind. Eddie had asked if I was interested in working for him as a sales representative for his printing company. I'd turned it down at the time but I re-approached him about it. He replied that the offer was still open and that he would agree to pay me as a company rather than employing me as an individual. That way I was getting some sort of security of income whilst I solicited other work for my promotions company. Provided I reached pre-set sales quotas, Eddie didn't mind what else I did.

The final thing which needed sorting out was the police. I explained the situation to them and they were also very understanding. After talking it through, they said that it wouldn't be held against me if I resigned and then applied again a few years later, because I'd already put in four and a half years of service.

I had nothing to lose. I could start the company, which was a pure 'speculator' whilst having the security of an income from Eddie. If it didn't work out, then I still had the option of rejoining the police. With everything sorted out in my head, I went back to Paul and Pat to hammer out an agreement about their involvement and how everybody would be paid.

While I was doing that, I had another meeting with one of the top men in the PR section of the police. Every time I'd done some promotional work for them, I'd come in contact with this guy. He admitted that I had been a great asset to them and that the PR work I'd done would have been very difficult to get elsewhere. He'd looked through General Instructions, the police bible, as I had, and seen that 'leave without pay' could only be given to those going overseas or into full-time education. However, he had spoken to some others in high ranking positions and, in view of what I had done for them, they were going to grant me twelve months sabbatical. Knowing how difficult it is in the police force to go against something etched in stone, such as the General Instructions, I knew that a lot of people must have put in a lot of effort to secure such an agreement and I was very thankful for it.

It took a while for people to get used to the fact that I was there in the market place for promotional work. However, work started to trickle in and gradually increased. It helped that I'd virtually reached Eddie's twelve-month target in the first five months, which gave me a lot of spare time to sell myself around. Most of the work centred around the same sort of things that I had been doing before, for free. There was the standard interviews, after-dinner speeches and guest appearances. Something that I quite liked was celebrity bar work, all I had to do was serve behind a bar and chat to people as they made their order.

The largest contract which I managed to pick up was with one of the local breweries. Basically it put me at their beck-and-call and I would turn up wherever they wanted me, say a promotional night in one of their pubs for a particular beer. However, that and all the other contracts were not for a great deal of money. Many people thought I must have been pocketing a small fortune, but that wasn't the case at all. Work, and therefore payments, came in dribs and drabs. Since there was a recession going on in New Zealand at the time, companies were cutting back on their promotional budgets.

I didn't find the work all that stimulating. At times it was a laugh but far from exciting. In any evening I would usually have to make the same idle conversation with a hundred different people and tell the same old stories. After the twentieth such evening, I started to get very tired of talking about myself. By the time I was approached by Leeds, I was starting to find it hard to motivate myself for the work. I would have carried on with it but I knew that it wasn't really for me.

Meanwhile, actually playing rugby was still the main part of my life, and I was picked for the New Zealand team to go to the Hong Kong Sevens. Arriving in the colony we found ourselves third favourites behind Australia and Fiji. It made a pleasant change to being out-and-out favourites and I found the lack of pressure very refreshing.

I'd never experienced anything quite like the atmosphere that pervaded during the competition. The place had a buzz which even surpassed the fifteen-a-side World Cup finals. In fact, the whole event seemed like one giant party. I also bumped into two players I'd known from Askeans days. They filled me in on what was happening back in Lewisham and made me feel a bit homesick for the first time in many a year.

In the competition itself, we got through our early pool games by scoring about forty points in both matches. Then we came up against Western Samoa in the quarter-final and had to fight for a 22-6 victory.

The semi-final was the hardest game we were to have. It was against the crowd favourites, Fiji. I've never been able to figure out just why they are the favourites when they persist with head-high tackles and are constantly maiming their opposition. But then I'm hardly unbiased. At the end of the first half we were down 0-10 and it looked like we were going out. Waisale Severi had a chance to put it beyond us with a break from deep in his own half. He went straight round Schuey and was set for a try. However, he was a bit overconfident and slowed down, giving me the chance to catch him and prevent the score. That signalled a turnabout in fortunes, and we scrapped a win in the last minute with a length of the pitch try by Dallas Seymour, 12-10.

The final against Australia was easy in comparison and we walked off with the trophy through a 22-10 win. Since we had won the tournament the hard way, by beating the favourites and the second favourites, being called the champions really made us feel as if we had achieved something.

Coming back on the plane I was celebrating with Zinny. He turned to me and said, "Here, Kipper, who have you got next week in the Nationals ?". I didn't know who we were playing so I replied, "Don't know Zinny, who have you got ?". He looked me in the eyes and smiled, "We've got you. Funny isn't it. Next week, I'll want to kill you !".

Trials were held again for the All Blacks at the start of the domestic test season and I reclaimed my full-back spot. There followed three very strenuous home series against France, Argentina and Australia.

We managed to beat the French 25-17 and 34-20 after they had given us a few frights. The thing that I remember most about the series was that the French refused to lie down and kept coming back at us. Also, Serge was kicking goals from everywhere. He isn't renowned for his penalty taking, but he slotted at least one over from fifty metres out.

Argentina were a little easier to handle and we beat them 60-9 and 49-12. In the first test I managed to get three tries, because there was nothing else to do. The forwards were in the ascendency for the whole game and I was required to do very little in defence. The second test was nearly the same and we scored a try from the kick off, with the ball passing through about ten pairs of hands. I only scored one try, but the game was more remarkable for me because it was the first time that I had played a test match in Wellington.

Australia came over for a single Bledisloe Cup game a week after Argentina had left, and we won by 24-12. The day before the game I got a call from the hotel reception saying that two cousins were waiting for me downstairs. When I went down I didn't even recognise them because they had changed so much. We sat and talked for a long time before they had to leave. When they'd gone I started to feel a bit homesick again. If my cousins had aged and grown up so much then my parents must be doing the same and I was missing out on their lives.

My cousins were in the middle of a holiday trip to Australia and New Zealand with their parents, my Uncle and Auntie. They all ended up coming back with me to Wellington and staying in my house. When we arrived, my Auntie expressed surprise as to the smallness of my home. She had expected me to be living in a mansion and driving a Porsche because I was a 'top' sportsman. Sadly, I had to enlighten her about her misconception and explain that we weren't paid the same as soccer players.

It had been a very busy period. I had played France three times in consecutive weeks, because Wellington had played them between the two tests. Straight afterwards we had played Argentina twice, followed by a week off and then the game against Australia. It was a bit like the World Cup series but obviously without the associated pressures and hype.

Right in the middle of it all, between the two Argentina tests, there had been a game arranged for an Anzac team. A combination of Australian and New Zealand players were to play the British Lions who had just beaten Australia in a series. I was asked to play, along with seven or eight other All Blacks, and I accepted. It was going to be something different, and I didn't know if I was ever going to get another chance to play against a British Lions side.

In the end I had to pull out because I had twinged a hamstring in the first test against Argentina on the heavy pitch at Dunedin. It wasn't too serious and I probably could have played but it would have been a risk. I thought long and hard about it but decided my priorities had to lie with the All Blacks. While the Anzac match was going to be a special game, it wasn't going to be a test.

Unfortunately some of the others thought the same way, for various reasons, and only three All Blacks ended up going to Ballymore for the game. It was a shame, and I can understand why some people got very upset about it. A few thought that there was a conspiracy in the All Black camp not to send anybody over but there wasn't.

Just to make sure we didn't get too much rest there was an end of season tour to Ireland and Wales. Realising that we were all tired, the selectors chose a squad of thirty players so there would be at least two who could play in any position. My 'cover' was Matthew Ridge who had joined the squad in the same situation as I had joined it on the tour of France. While I had been Kieran's understudy, Matthew was going to be mine. The feeling was odd; I was only twenty-five with plenty of rugby left in me but here was a twenty-year old being groomed for my place. Was I getting old or were the other players getting younger ? The tour was always going to be something special for me because I was actually going back to Britain as a seasoned All Black. But I didn't realise just how it was going to affect me.

On the way over we stopped off in Canada and had a pleasant stay. While we were there, we were interviewed by a reporter from the Rugby World & Post magazine who had come out to cover the game and quiz us about professionalism in the sport. He ended up giving us a fair hearing and I quite liked the article that he produced. However, he warned us that the press in the UK were going to hit us hard on the professionalism bit. Buck, JK and myself were going to get most of it because we all had our own promotions companies. It didn't worry me at all because I'd done everything within the rules. They could ask me whatever questions they liked but I had nothing to hide.

Sure enough, as soon as we walked through customs at Heathrow the press were waiting for us, and we were confronted by a barrage of questions from reporters trying to stir up trouble. Buck took most of the flack because he had decided to do some promotional work in the UK, while JK and I had decided not to.

After a morning in London we flew straight up to Cardiff to get on with the rugby. I entered the tour feeling a little sorry for the Welsh. The country had been in an economic depression for a number of years but they had always managed to keep their heads up with a certain pride in their rugby. However, they had been on the receiving end of a couple of good hidings in New Zealand, and things weren't looking good for them in the foreseeable future, with so many defections to Rugby League. Our strength had come from keeping our team together whilst the Welsh had been decimated. Admittedly, there had also been some managerial and hierarchial problems in Wales. But Scotland had the same problems and yet managed to produce a good side by keeping an essentially consistent team.

The lack of spirit in the Welsh team also showed up in the test match. Whilst there was a sense of urgency and pride in the club sides like Llanelli, Neath, Cardiff and Swansea it seemed to be lacking in the national squad. With the All Blacks always being capable of lifting their game, the test result was never in any doubt.

John's dad was following the tour and rang me with some tickets for the Llanelli game. I gratefully accepted and agreed to meet Sean Gallagher outside the temporary stand especially erected for this match. I duly got up at 5 a.m. on the Saturday in question, looking forward to watching my old mate for the first time since his selection for the All Blacks. It was a terrible morning but I drove the two hundred-odd miles listening to the radio for reports on the game. The first thing I heard, when sitting in a queue of traffic to the Severn Bridge (shortly before its closure), was an announcement on 'Sport on Four' of the New Zealand team for the day "...at number 15 Matthew Ridge in place of John Gallagher" - marvellous!

I carried on regardless thinking that we would be able to have a laugh together during the game. I made my detour via Swansea to collect the tickets from a white plastic swan that had been left on a doorstep and eventually arrived at the ground: The temporary stand had been closed due to the storm. The rain was incessant - quite the worst day of the year and no Sean Gallagher. I ended up watching the game from the terrace, on my own, soaked to the skin. All I could see was this smug ginger idiot all wrapped up nice and warm in the Directors Box.

I had no idea where they were staying so at the end of the game I rushed over and started to shout up at him, only to be told by a camera man "Go away Sonny". I told the camera man what to do with his zoom lens and went to the players entrance looking extremely smart by this stage. I eventually got to the changing rooms from where Gallagher emerged and the bugger didn't even recognise me. My only comment was, "What a mate".

KIERAN MASTERSON

Many of the All Blacks, including myself, had dreamed about playing at Cardiff Arms Park. And the reality proved to be as vivid as those dreams. When the Welsh anthem was sung by the entire crowd it was like a force attacking me from every angle and it raised the hairs on the back of my neck. There was a huge cauldron of passion being aroused and it certainly intimidated us.

However, the writing was on the wall within the first few minutes when Craig Innes, standing in for the injured JK, came from the blind to the open side of a scrum five metres out and was pushed over by the loose forwards for a try. The Welsh then rallied and held us up for about twenty minutes but finally capitulated to a 34-9 defeat.

After the game we were sitting in the changing rooms when I heard a bit of a commotion and a familiar voice. Mum had missed my passing through London so she had been determined to come to Cardiff. Having watched the game she had decided that she was going to come down and see me. I don't know how she got past the security or avoided Grizz, but she did and waltzed in to the changing rooms as if she was one of the players. A few of the boys thought that she was the St Johns Ambulance woman and let her through. She came straight over to me and gave me a hug and a kiss. It was lovely to see her but I simply wanted to die. No woman had ever been in the All Blacks changing rooms before and I felt like an embarrassed kid getting a kiss from his Mum at the school gates. To make matters worse, Peter Bush was on hand with his camera and he pushed through to get a shot which was to appear on the front page of some of the national newspapers in New Zealand !

A sad thing about the Welsh arm of the tour was the attitude of some of the crowd at the club games. I don't want to over generalise, but we were spat on and abused for most of the eighty minutes against Llanelli and Neath every time we went near the touchline. The pitiful thing about it, is that youngsters watching the older ones will probably grow up thinking that spitting is the right thing to do and copy that appalling behaviour. I'd never ever come across it before and quite a few of my team-mates were shocked. In addition, there were also a couple of occasions when the referee was physically attacked at the end of the game for giving a decision against the home side. Not a good omen.

From Wales we went straight on to Ireland. Here we found a different way of life. There was no abuse at the games or in the streets, and everybody we met seemed more relaxed about their rugby. On the pitch, though, it was a different story. Munster became the first team to stand up to us during the Haka by glaring at us from the half-way line. Having roused themselves that far, they continued their aggression into the game and tore at us as if their lives depended on the result. I could have sworn that I saw smoke coming out of their ears. The tackling was a lot more ferocious than we had encountered anywhere in Wales and they took the game to us for the whole of the match.

Thousands of spectators turned up to watch the game, far more than the ground could take, and unfortunately some didn't get in at all. The noise wasn't as deafening as Cardiff Arms had been but it was loud nonetheless. Despite this, and instead of abusing us, they treated us with respect such as applauding good moves. It was most noticeable every time Foxy was taking a kick, the whole ground fell deadly silent so that he could concentrate.

The next day we were travelling north to Galway and the plan was to stop at the Young Munster's rugby club in Limerick for a light lunch. It was only a stones-throw from my Grandmothers house and she turned up to see me with the press in tow. She was eighty-seven going on eighty-eight at the time but the sweet thing was she told the press she was only eighty-five. Obviously women fib about their age for their entire lives. But was great to see her again and we had quite an emotional reunion.

At the same time the rest of the boys had become involved with some of the Limerick locals and had acquired a taste for the lazy style of life. Guinness also seemed to rest well with their kama and the one hour stopover turned into an elongated four hour session. It was that sort of spontaneous and soothing time which made us sad when we eventually had to leave Ireland.

The emotion on the Irish pitches continued into the test. Just like at the start of the Munster match, the Irish side all came up to the half-way line and stared at us doing the Haka. Then, as we were sticking our tongues out, wiggling our hands and jumping up-and-down, I noticed that they had linked arms and were advancing in a 'V' shape into our ranks. None of us knew what was going on and you could feel the tension in the air mounting towards some sort of crescendo. I was stood right on the end and looked across to see Kieran Crossan, the winger, looking at me. He smiled and then started laughing which set me off. Meanwhile Willie Anderson had dragged the point of the 'V' well into our crescent and was coming eyeball-to-eyeball with Buck and Steve McDowell. Everybody was going red in the face and a punch-up looked to be on the cards. Kieran and I thought it was a bit of fun but the others obviously didn't think so.

Fortunately the Haka ended and, after a short but noticeable pause, everybody dispersed with fire in their bellies. Afterwards, Buck and the rest said that they thought it was a good challenge, but I'm just thankful the Irish didn't touch anybody or come further into the crescent. If they had then anybody could guess what would have happened. As it was they came right to the edge, had a look and let us know they were there. As if we were in any doubt, Willie Anderson turned around and started throwing his arms up into the air, getting the crowd going.

With a start like that there is no way that it was going to be a jaunt of a game. The tackling was deadly and space in which to move was at a premium. The crowd also sensed the intensity and cheered for the whole game. Even as the Irish fell behind and when it looked certain that they would lose, the spectators kept cheering. This was another contrast to Wales where, even at Cardiff Arms Park, the crowds had fallen quiet as soon as it became apparent the home side was heading for defeat.

I thoroughly enjoyed the game and it was all the more enjoyable because a lot of my family and relatives were in the stands. As luck would have it, I scored possibly my best try ever for the All Blacks. There was a scrum on half-way, with a fifteen metre blind-side on the right, so we went open to the left. Graeme Bachop gave the first pass to Foxy, who missed out Schuey and sent it straight on to Bullet. I was running alongside him but he missed me out and gave the ball to Terry Wright. Automatically we had an overlap, Terry drew the winger and I looped round for the pass. With the ball and only daylight in front of me, I headed for the line. On the way I sensed the other winger coming across and I could tell that he was going to 'corner flag' me. Without getting a good look at him I went off my left foot, slowing slightly but not losing my stride, and stepped inside him. From there it was a straight sprint for the try-line. Little did I know at the time that it was to be my last try for the All Blacks.

When we arrived back in England, we also arrived back in the rat-race. After the tranquil and enjoyable time in Ireland we were thrown straight into the usual hassles. More press, more photographs and more 'sensational' stories about what we were 'earning' appeared in the tabloids.

There was a lot of exaggeration and muck raked up about us 'walking out' of a reception 'thrown in our honour'. In reality, we had arrived in London the morning after a late game the night before in Ulster, and then we'd been whisked off to the Café Royal for this luncheon. Nobody really knew what was going on and when we got there we were all split up onto different tables. I was lucky because I had some interesting people on my table, but others had a very hard time making small-talk with some small-minded people. Everybody was very tired and we were still in our travelling clothes. So, after sitting politely through the speeches, we got together, excused ourselves and left. We needed to get showered, changed and, if possible, get a training run in since we were playing the Barbarians in a couple of days.

The inaccurate reporting which followed really wound me, and a few of the others, up the wrong way. As far as I was concerned we were there to play rugby not be shown-off like a herd of prize bulls. That form of hassle by the media didn't happen anywhere else. In France, Australia, Hong Kong, Canada and Ireland we were treated like rugby players, but in England and Wales the media constantly tried to knock us down.

One of the main highlights of returning to London, for some of the team, came when we were taken to meet the Queen. As we walked in to The Palace, I could tell everybody was even more nervous than before a big game. We were led from the inner courtyard, along a red carpet, up a long flight of stairs into a waiting room. The route was lined with paintings of previous Kings and Queens, and the waiting room itself looked like an art gallery. After a few minutes we were taken into The White Room where we were told the Queen would be along in a few minutes. This room was a bit more spartan than the first, with a really high roof and, what looked like, two gold painted dressing tables at either end.

We stood talking amongst ourselves for what seemed like ages, constantly wiping sweaty hands on our trousers. Eventually the Queen was announced by one of the ushers and, to my amazement, she stepped out from one of the 'dressing tables'. I was also taken aback by her height. Having merely seen her on TV, I didn't realise that she was only about five feet three inches tall. In fact her first remark to us as a group was "My goodness, how big you all are !". After an initial welcoming speech, we broke up into groups of three or four, and she came to each group for a longer chat. When she talked to the group I was in, I thought she came across more like a really nice lady than the head of the realm.

The following day, we met her daughter when we were all introduced to Princess Anne on the pitch before our game against the Barbarians. She must have read something about me before, because she shook my hand, moved on to those further down the line and then came back saying, "I suppose this is a bit of a homecoming for you isn't it ?". I thought it flattering that she recognised me, and I had a smile on my face throughout the game.

The Baabaas scored early on and stayed in front right up to half time. It took us until half way through the second half before we regained the lead, and then Richard Loe scored the try which sealed the game for us.

In the baths afterwards we were discussing the game when I started to reflect on my rugby. All of a sudden I realised that I had done everything I wanted to in Rugby Union; I'd got into the All Blacks, toured France, won the World Cup, toured Australia and come out as top try scorer, been awarded the New Zealand player-of-the-year, won the Hong Kong Sevens, scored possibly my best try in front of the family in Ireland, played at Cardiff Arms Park and played the Baabaas at Twickenham. In a way I'd come full circle, back to that fateful day when I made an idiot of myself in the Middlesex Sevens at the same ground. What else was there left to do ?

Chapter 14

The World's Best Rugby Player ?

The year 1990 started much the same for me as any other, but it wasn't going to follow the same course. I was invited out to participate in the Western Samoan international club sevens tournament. I'd been once before but ended up spending a lot of time on the toilet, because there had been some flooding and the drinking water had been infected. As a result I'd only seen the country through a bamboo skylight, so I'd vowed to return.

My invitation came from the host club Marist-St Josephs. Buck had also been persuaded to go over to the same club, but not to play, only to help with the coaching. Of course, as these things go, once safely in their clubhouse, they set about persuading him to take to the pitch and succeeded.

Buck and I took the club for a preliminary training session and we agreed that we were up against it. There wasn't a lot of cohesion in the side. But looking at the opposition in our pool, we reckoned that we might be able to get through and reach the quarter finals on the second day. If we could get that far, then we thought we would have warranted our trip out.

Things went to plan, and by the pool games we had cemented a bit of discipline into the team. Game by game they seemed to get better and we walked through each contest to qualify for the next day. In the quarters we were drawn against the national side from Raratonga. We thought they would give us some trouble, but we managed to beat them quite comfortably. That put us into the semi-final and the whole crowd was getting behind us because we were representing the host club.

Our semi was against a side from the Fiji Police, which had half of the Fiji national squad playing for it. They were the favourites to reach the final and nobody expected us to progress any further. As if he thought he was in a test match, Buck really started to get going and he took on everybody in sight, which gave me plenty to feed from. In addition, the Samoan lads responded to the way we were playing, and stepped up their game to become totally unrecognisable from the ones who started. We won and we knew that we were entering the final with a good side. Both Buck and I left the pitch laughing our heads off.

Our opposition in the final were the champions Moata'a. Fortunately for us their star player, Michael Jones, was still out with the knee injury which he'd picked up against Argentina. But they still had a side to be respected which included someone called Lolani Koko. They had a great start and scored after two minutes, and I thought we were going to go down to a heavy defeat. However, we managed to score and then exchanged another couple of tries to finish the first half level pegging. Then in the second half, I remember running alongside Buck who had the ball and was intent on collecting as many opposition as possible. In the end he had four of them hanging off him, but still managed to keep going and throw out a pass to one of the team who scored. That proved to be the decisive score and we won the whole tournament.

We were happy, but not as happy as the ten thousand locals who had turned up to watch. The after-match function turned into a huge party and everybody was going wild over our victory. Schuey, who had been playing for his Wellington club side Marist-St Pats, was made into a High Chief to follow on from his grandfather. He was given the title Chief Solea which bestowed on him a local status similar to a knighthood. Because everybody knew I was great mates with Schuey, plus the fact that I'd been made player-of-the-tournament, they decided to make me a minor Chief. There wasn't time to prepare a proper ceremony, but I was named Honorary Chief Toi. The full ritual was supposed to take place the following year in 1991 when I said I was going to return. Unfortunately I couldn't attend because I was in equally exotic Warrington at the time.

My first impressions of John were, I suppose, that he was a fair player for someone who had just broken on to the Wellington rep scene. But, over that first year he started to impress me as a player of immense talent. The ability to take a high ball under pressure, run into the backline with devastating pace and his overall game, seemed to shine apart from the rest of his colleagues. It wasn't long until he was selected for the team to wear the Silver Fern. I suppose most of the rugby nation could see his supreme ability as an attacking fullback.

One memory that stands out was our little trip to Samoa to play Sevens. Kipper and I were invited to play for the local rugby club St Joseph's. John and I spent most of our time organising the Samoan boys. What we did with them must have worked, because we made it all the way to the final, eventually winning in a hard fought battle against Michael Jones' team Moata'a.

After the presentation, John and the team jumped on the back of an old Landrover. They must have driven around town for an hour holding the cup high in the air rejoicing in a good win. The funny thing was, it was so hot nobody had shirts on and on the back of the truck were ten or so Samoans and a Pom, who looked like a bloody red lobster, all throwing down beer as if it was going out of fashion. It was a good week-end for both of us.
WAYNE SHELFORD

Schuey and I were both picked again to play in the Hong Kong Sevens. Things went well and we got through to the semi-final stage fairly easily. At this point we met the Barbarians but managed to see them off 24-6.

In the final we faced Fiji and we cruised to a 10-0 lead before they scored, to make it 10-6 at half time. Then in the second half, I had a forty metre run down the sideline but got bundled into touch just after half-way. As the Fijians prepared to take the ensuing line-out, I went to rush back into my position at centre. However, the ball was thrown in quickly and Schuey called for me to stay where I was; he would cover my position. The plan was to rush the Fijians, taking them man-for-man, which would give them the overlap but we would be so quick that they would fumble the ball.

The first pass came out high to Waisale Serevi, and we rushed up to crowd them out. Waisale saw Schuey coming and simply tapped the ball on its way straight over his head with both hands. Because it was an uncontrolled pass, it fell low to the next Fijian who was standing square on to the ball and who caught it by his ankles. In one movement he flicked it between his legs before Terry Wright hit him, and it landed plumb into the hands of Tomasi Cama. He had about fifty metres to go to the line and I was the only one left to cover him. About five metres short, I thought I had him, but he stepped off his outside foot and cut inside me. With my legs still awash with lactic acid from my recent run, they refused to turn and just buckled below me. Tomasi made no mistake and finished off the best try I have ever seen in Sevens to make it 10-12 against us. From then on we squandered a few openings and they came in to score two late tries and to make the final score 10-22. There were no excuses, we had been beaten by some extremely good play.

The following day, the team got together in the Bull & Bear pub, next to the Hilton where we were staying, for a celebratory drink. We decided to have a court session and Schuey was made the judge. We were well into it, and we had all downed a few penalties for wearing bright socks or similar misdemeanours, when an English guy came over. He said he thought we had played skilfully, and that it was a bit of a shame about losing the final. Because we had done so well he would like to buy us a jug of beer. Naturally we accepted and offered him our thanks. The jug arrived and was placed on my side of the table (I was sitting on one side of Schuey, with Zinny on the other). The others were all drinking from different jugs. The session continued with Zinny and myself getting most of the fines on our side, and Schuey doing most of the talking but having the occasional drink.

After about only an hour-and-a-half in the pub, we went back to the hotel to get changed and pack for the flight home. None of us thought we were particularly drunk because, in total, we had only had about three pints each. However, as we left the pub, Zinny fell over and had to be carried back to the hotel in a real mess. By the time we reached the hotel I was feeling hot and cold but went upstairs to get changed. Meanwhile Zinny had gone up to his room and was throwing up blood in the shower.

Once changed, I came down to wait for the bus and stood talking to some of the boys from New Zealand Television. They looked at me and said that I didn't look well. No sooner had they made that comment, and I'd started to protest my innocence at drinking too much, then I started to throw up blood as well into one of the foyer pot plants. They took me back upstairs to recover...

Fourteen hours later, I woke up ! Zinny was lying next to me on a huge crispy-white bed and he woke up about the same time. Through the incessant thumping in my head, I focused on an official from the Hong Kong Rugby Union who had stayed with us all night. Apparently an expatriate doctor had been in, examined us, given us jabs and said that we had been poisoned with something like ether.

Schuey hadn't drunk much from the jug and went with the others on the flight back to New Zealand. But evidently he was a real handful on the plane, taking over the demonstration of the lifejacket and generally being a pain. The others had just thought he was very drunk and forced him to sit down. He then fell asleep for ten hours.

Nobody else was ill apart from Zinny, Schuey and myself. The only thing we had done differently from the rest was drink from that jug which had been bought for us by a 'well wisher'. There was obviously something fishy about it. I don't think it had been a malicious attempt to kill us, or anything that sinister. More likely, it was a prank which had repercussions well beyond what was expected.

Having fully recovered, I was sitting at home in Wellington one evening in late March watching 'Eastenders' on the telly when I heard the 'phone ringing. I was deeply engrossed in the programme so I contemplated not answering. However, the caller was persistent, so I relented, and picked up the receiver.

"Can I speak to John Gallagher, please," a voice said.

"Speaking," I replied, thinking the press were after me again.

"My name is Bernard Colby, from Leeds Rugby League Football Club in England. I've been following your progress in rugby and I've read in the newspapers that you may be interested in moving to play Rugby League," the voice continued.

"No you haven't," I replied fairly aggressively, "because I've never said anything like that to anybody".

"Well would you be interested," Bernard persisted.

"To be honest with you, I haven't given it much thought but I am curious. I wouldn't want to say 'No' to you over the 'phone without learning a bit more about the game".

"OK, well how about I send you over a ticket and you can come and see us this week or the week after..."

"Hang on a minute," I interjected, "you've only been on the 'phone for five minutes and already you want me to fly over ?"

Bernard explained that they had actually been trying to get hold of me the year before, but the only way they could contact me was through Rugby Union circles. This time they had used a contact in Auckland Rugby League to find out my home 'phone number. So, they had been thinking about trying to sign me for considerably longer than five minutes.

Still I couldn't accept his offer of tickets. I'd just been made captain of Wellington by the new coach, Andy Leslie, in my seventh season playing for them. It was a great honour; I was the first Englishman to have been given the position in the history of the long-established Union. Having games every week it would've needed a really good excuse for me to be absent, and I didn't think 'checking out' a Rugby League club was sufficient. My name would have been mud. Instead, I pointed out that I'd recently received a 'phone call from Nigel Starmer-Smith of Rugby World & Post saying that I'd been voted 'International Player of the Year'. The ceremony was going to take place in London and I was going to come over for a week starting 6th May, so that would provide an opportunity for me to come up and see the club. The conversation ended with me giving him my parents 'phone number and saying that if he was still interested, then to give me a call when I was over.

I'd planned my trip to London to fall between playing for Wellington against New South Wales in the South Pacific Championship on Sunday 6th May and against Wanganui on Tuesday 15th May. On the morning of the New South Wales game, a letter dropped on the doorstep. I sort of half recognised the writing, and on opening it I realised it was from Anita, my ex-girlfriend in Lewisham. Instead of writing back, I decided to give her a call when I was in London.

Straight after the game I flew back to London and arrived on Monday 7th, because you gain a day when flying to England from New Zealand. On the Monday night, I gave Anita a call and arranged to see her on Wednesday for which she had to take a day off from teaching at a local school. I also called Kieran to set up a chat and a few beers for Thursday. That virtually filled my timetable because, with losing a day flying back, I had to leave on Sunday 13th.

Tuesday came, and I received my International Player of the Year award, with Mum and Dad present, at the Whitbread brewery in London. We had a really good day and were well looked after. I received my tankard along with Brian Moore who got the 'British Player of the Year' and Tony Stanger who got the 'Most Promising Player of the Year'. Naturally, you would think that the International award would be the most prestigious but, since it was the first year that the International award had been given, my tankard was by far the smallest trophy.

All five nominations for the award came from the All Black ranks; there was Buck, Foxy, Gary Whetton, Steve McDowell and myself. The final selection was made by the combination of a readers vote and the views of a panel. Plenty of press came along and, as I'd come to expect, the write-ups got out of hand. I was hailed as the 'World's Best Full-back' and, more sensationally, 'The World's Best Rugby Player'. The 'titles' probably came about because I had been voted as the best player in what was undoubtedly the world's best team at the time, the All Blacks. But the title never really sat easy on my mind.

So many things go to make up a good player. I was very fortunate to be part of a team which allowed me to play my particular brand of rugby. I don't think I would have got into the English or Irish teams, but if I had my running and attacking game would not have fitted in so well. Similarly, if the All Blacks team pattern had been one of ten-man rugby then you can be pretty sure that the world would not have heard of John Gallagher. As it was, our plans were always to play fifteen-man rugby and that allowed me to come to the fore. But to say that I was any better than anyone else in the All Black side would be ridiculous. I've always considered myself to be a good team member and I've always buckled down to do my job. Of course I was very flattered to be voted ahead of the others but I still think that it is a team sport with the emphasis on 'team'. Without the skills of the others I would never have had the chance to score any of my tries.

As for being the best full-back, I don't know how Serge Blanco and David Campese were overlooked. Serge is simply a fantastic free spirit on the pitch. When he is on-song, which is most of the time, he is superb. A natural athlete, he reads the game like nobody else and can completely take the opposition apart if he sees a weakness. He can also run like a gazelle, which makes him dangerous from anywhere on the field. Running with ball-in-hand is definitely his strong point, and any defence better not take their eyes off him for a moment or he'll be past them before they know it. Perhaps he didn't get the award in 1989/90 because he didn't have a very good domestic season, I don't know. But there is no doubt he has been the best full-back during the 80's, and receiving the 1990/91 award is some sort of recompense. I would like to think that if I'd stayed around for a few more years, then maybe I'd have been able to compare myself with him.

Having said that, I'm not sure if Serge, or for that matter David Campese, would have 'made it' in the All Blacks. No doubt their individual skills would have got them into the team but their strengths lie in being unpredictable. That would have been knocked out of them in the New Zealand team. They would have become better players but less flamboyant. The All Blacks don't need anybody doing stupid things behind their own goal line and running the ball out. They want players who will play consistent percentage rugby all of the time and then pull something extra out of the bag when given a chance. As a result I think they would have both had to change their games so much they may not have stood out. Discipline comes first with the All Blacks and flair is just an added bonus. There will never be any room for an individual in their side.

The 'titles' also took no notice of Rugby League, as is the Rugby Union way. I'd been slightly educated in League by watching Australian games and a few of the English matches on TV. There were obviously many outstanding players such as Wally Lewis, Garry Schofield, Mal Meninga and Ellery Hanley all of whom would have a claim to the title 'World's Best Rugby Player'. However, I saw them as playing a different game. People usually only consider Rugby Union players in Rugby League and say, "Oh, he did well, but the other one didn't". Nobody ever considers the other way around. Where, for instance, would you play Mal Meninga in Union ? His best position would probably be at centre, but what is his kicking game like which is very important in Union ? Ever since the two codes started to go their own way in 1895 the differences have been there. As a result, League has had its good players and Union has had its own. The two sets should not be compared.

In short, being given the tag of 'World's Rugby Best player', albeit by the media, was very very flattering and I'll always look back on it with pride. But there is no way that I can accept it.

The next day, Wednesday, I took Anita out in Mike's car to Brighton. We had a very agreeable day and did a lot of chatting about old times. I thought it was obvious we both still liked one another but neither of us was really letting on verbally. As far as both of us were concerned, this was a one-off trip and I'd soon be returning to New Zealand.

When John called to say he was in London and that he wanted to take me out on Wednesday, I initially said, "No". At that point of my life, I was living for my work as a Geography teacher and I was really busy. However, John finished the conversation by saying, "Right I'll see you at half-nine then" and putting the phone down. I didn't know what to do, so I explained the situation to my Head of Department, who said I'd be daft if I didn't see John.

So, I called in sick on the Wednesday morning and waited for him to arrive. At nine-thirty on the dot, which is incredibly unusual for somebody like John, he drew up outside in a lovely green MG. I thought 'this is looking good' because I'd always wanted one myself. Then John got out of the car and he was looking better than I'd remembered. I could tell from that point on that the day was going to go from strength-to-strength.

I greeted him as an 'old friend' and we chugged off to Brighton with the MG making one hell of a row. Once there, we just strolled around the town looking in shops and visiting the pier. All the time we were chattering away and I found myself liking him more and more. To my delight, John started walking backwards, in front of me but looking at me, which I intuitively took to mean he was thinking the same thoughts.

On the way home, I shifted through Mike's tapes in the car and put on the Eagles 'Johnny come lately', which we'd always played when we were in the sixth-form. Back at home on my own in the evening, I thought 'what a lovely day' and went to bed thinking very hard about the future, and John.
ANITA

By Thursday I had given up on hearing from Leeds. They had known when I was going to be in London and that time was going to be tight. Because there hadn't been a call, I reckoned that they must have changed their minds about wanting me. Thinking no more of it, I got changed and prepared to go out with Kieran and his brother for a few drinks in the evening. Just as I was about to leave the 'phone rang. It was Bernard Colby again. He said that he was coming down to London for the FA cup final on the Saturday and asked if I wanted to see him there to discuss a possible move. I replied honestly, that I didn't think it was worth it, because such a meeting in a London hotel wasn't going to answer any of my questions. I wanted to see the club itself and judge from that. He said that he understood my thinking and offered to meet me in Leeds on Friday, with the coach David Ward; to which I agreed.

In the pub that evening I confided in Kieran, and Ralph, his brother-in-law who had come along for a drink, about what was going on. Kieran seemed more astounded by the fact that I intended to go up on my own, rather than by the fact that I was considering changing codes. "You can't go up by yourself," he said "Look, I'll come up with you and pretend to be your agent !". I laughed and told him that Bernard would see straight through him. He tried to persuade me otherwise but I was having nothing of it.

Ralph had been listening to the conversation with interest. He was a few years older than both of us and had been an accountant in the city for some time. He butted in and said that Kieran had a point, I couldn't go up on my own in case I was talked in to doing something that I didn't want to do. Instead, he thought it might be better if he came along. This offer I accepted. Ralph seemed to have a wiser head on his shoulders and would be able to talk the same language as the Leeds money-men. It was nice of him to offer because he had to cancel several meetings in the city to make the trip.

We met at Kings Cross the following morning and took the train direct to Leeds. On the way up, Ralph asked me what my decision was likely to be. I said that I had been thinking about it ever since Bernard's first 'phone call, and if Leeds could agree on terms then I saw no reason why I shouldn't give it a go. Every year I'd been setting myself targets in Rugby Union, and 1990 had been the first season I'd had to start without a clearly defined goal. As far as I could tell, I'd done everything and I was in need of a new challenge. Having followed Australian Rugby League on TV it looked like a fast, physical, entertaining game and I thought that it would provide me with the challenge I was looking for.

Two other factors had swayed me towards the idea of accepting the Leeds offer if it was good enough. Over Christmas I'd realised that my parents weren't getting any younger and that I'd been missing from their lives for a considerable period. Time was running out to rectify the situation. I was also in need of some security. The promotional work was providing me with some income but nothing substantial. I was aware that the trickle of work that existed, would dry up the moment I became unpopular perhaps as the result of one bad game. At the age of twenty-six, I had to start looking towards the future.

Thinking more about the monetary aspects, I had come up with a figure which I thought I was worth. It was based on my estimate of how long I had left to play, and what I would need to set myself up with the basics in England. By many people's standards it might have been called a considerable sum, but I don't think its generally realised how much it costs to set up even a small home from scratch in a new country. If I could have been sure of playing until I was 75 then it might have been lower.

Essentially, I was viewing the switch as a career move rather than jumping 'the great divide'. I was putting it on the same level as David Kirk giving up the captaincy of the All Blacks to go to Oxford University and on into business. Obviously some people were going to call me a traitor, and say that I was committing a heinous crime, but I was sure my friends would see it for what it was.

Bernard and David picked us up at the station and took us straight to Leeds' ground at Headingley. Being the off-season, they were sure that nobody would see me. At the club, I was quickly shown around and then taken up to the board room for lengthy discussions about the possibilities.

I was given a very professional presentation of what the city was like, what the club was like, what they were aiming for and where I would fit in. There weren't any view graphs or videos, but I was told most of what I wanted to know, very efficiently. Both Bernard and David added that they thought I would make a very good Rugby League player. Since they gave me the impression of being honest men and I liked what I had seen of the club, I was convinced that Leeds could provide my missing challenge. That only left the monetary negotiations.

As it turned out, my calculation of what I would need and their estimate of my worth were similar. Ralph handled most of the discussions with Bernard, about what should and what should not be put into the contract, since we had covered most of the possible scenarios on the train up.

A couple of little extra points came up while they were talking. Firstly, Bernard offered to let me see out the New Zealand domestic season. I declined that option on the basis that I couldn't play any form of Rugby Union knowing that I was going to sign for a Rugby League club. My heart wouldn't have been in what I was doing, and I wouldn't have been able to look anybody straight in the eye. Secondly, he pointed out that most of the players had jobs outside of their rugby, and he offered to help find me a job in Leeds. That was also a nice offer, but I had given it some thought and decided that I would like to go to college, picking up on the education I'd thrown away with my 'A'-level failures.

The negotiations ended with us all shaking hands and agreeing we were happy with the contract as discussed. However, they said that they couldn't finalise anything until they had been back to their board. That suited me because it was going to give me a bit more time to sort things out before the news hit the media.

Back in London, I told the details of the discussions and of the contract to Mum and Dad. I said I had a good feeling about the club and, if everything was put in writing, I was going to sign. They were both aware of my situation back in New Zealand, and of how much work I'd put in to reach my existing status, but they were both very supportive. Dad and I had a long discussion and he concluded by saying, "Well you've got to do it, haven't you !".

On the plane home, I suddenly thought about Anita. I hadn't told her anything about the Leeds approach or the possibility of me coming back to England. So I started to write her a letter, explaining everything and letting slip my true feelings about her. Unbeknown to me, she was about to write me a similar letter saying that she was all set to come for a long holiday to New Zealand. Our one day together had triggered off quite a lot. While there must have been something there all along, building up over the years, we had both been too afraid of our emotions to let them be known. It's funny how you know when you've met the right person.

I got John's letter via Los Angeles because he'd given it to an air-hostess to post, probably assuming she was coming back to the UK. I recognised his writing and opened it to see it said all the things I'd been thinking, but in a much more 'direct' way. I took a big gulp and thought I'd better write back immediately. Whereas John's letter to me had been about four hundred words long, the one I sent him covered five sides of A4 paper. In it I told him that I felt the same way about him, and that I was going to save up to visit him during my summer holidays.

ANITA

Chapter 15

The Chase

I got back to Wellington on Tuesday 15th and switched on the TV for a few minutes before I went to bed. To my utter amazement the news was filled with a story about Matthew Ridge signing for Manly Rugby League club in Australia. One of the reasons he gave, was he couldn't see himself getting into the All Black test side for a few years because I had the full-back position sewn up. I was stunned for a few moments, and started thinking if there was anything I could have done to let him know what I was planning. But even to this day, I'm sure there was nothing. After all, when I learned about his defection, I still hadn't actually signed.

Still feeling uncomfortable with myself the next day, I turned up as usual for the bus to Wanganui with the Wellington team. I tried to act as normal as possible during the day, but with a lot of talk on the bus about Matthew I was beginning to feel the pressure and get paranoid about anybody finding out my intentions. There was a bit of a release from my worries when we stopped at a hotel for a light refreshment before the game. Allan Hewson had made the journey, on his own, to watch the game. I started chatting to him and the topic of conversation inevitably turned to Matthew's defection. While discussing the 'rights' and 'wrongs', Allan said to me, "Well, if you get the chance to turn professional, you have to do it don't you ?". Obviously he didn't know what I was going through, but it helped to put my mind at ease a bit, knowing that he probably would have made the same decision as I had.

The game came and went with us recording a 39-0 victory. Surprisingly, I enjoyed the game and felt relaxed on the pitch, probably because we were given a lot of space to try out new moves. However, the tension returned on the drive home. I was sat at the front with Andy Leslie and Don Bond who were both giving me 'furtive' looks. At separate points on the journey, they both asked me if I was feeling alright because I looked even whiter than usual and was acting very quietly. My nerves nearly cracked, but I palmed everything off on the ubiquitous 'jet-lag'.

I desperately wanted to tell both of them as my friends, but also I didn't want to put either of them in a compromising position. My thinking was: If I did spill the beans, and they were questioned about my intentions, they would be torn between loyalty to the Union and breaking the confidence I would have bestowed in them. On top of everything, I still had a fear of the deal falling through. If it did, and I'd declared an intention to turn professional, my whole way of life would have been ruined. It was a very difficult decision, but, in the end, I decided silence was the best policy.

On Thursday 17th, I had a two-day engagement with Sky Television which had been arranged prior to my involvement with Leeds. They wanted to record some footage and to generally prepare for my part in their rugby coverage, even though I hadn't formally signed a contract with them. In addition there was going to be a 'Sky Launch' party. Again I was faced with the same dilemma; should I tell them it was unlikely I would be able to participate in the programmes as planned, or stay quiet in case everything fell through. I decided, if there had been anybody at Sky who I could have trusted to keep the secret, I would have told them, so they could have saved some expense and embarrassment. But my distrust of some aspects of the media was deep seated and based on experience, so I said nothing.

I knew if Leeds came up with the goods, I was going to need some help, which meant telling at least a couple of people. Firstly, I told Terry O'Connor who I'd taken in as a lodger to help pay the mortgage; I was going to need his help in redirecting any 'phone calls which might arrive for me while I was out of the house. Secondly, I told Lindsay Cunningham who was the accountant at Eddie's printing company; he was a friend of mine from Ories but just as importantly, at the time, he was used to dealing with contracts. I also tried to contact Schuey, who had missed the Wanganui game with an injury, but he had gone 'walkabout' somewhere.

With Terry and Lindsay's help enlisted, I set off for Auckland and the Sky TV studios. Thursday's filming went well, even though I felt ill at ease, and we had reached lunchtime of Friday's session when I received a call at the hotel. Terry had redirected a call from Leeds. It was Alf Davies who had taken over from Bernard Colby, who had himself resigned. That news was a bit of a shock, but Alf told me that the directors had approved my terms. He added that Leeds didn't want me to say anything about the deal, but to fly to Leeds for the signing where a press conference would be arranged. I replied that I was still happy with the agreement, but I couldn't come over to Leeds for the signing because there were a lot of people in New Zealand who I owed it to, to tell them first. I also didn't want to make the journey, to have everything fall through at the last minute and be exposed in front of the media. Fortunately, Alf saw my point of view and said that he would arrange for David Ward to fly out with the contract and meet me at 5 p.m. on Monday 21st (poor David was actually preparing to fly to Spain with the Leeds team for an end-of-season holiday but got redirected on the tarmac).

My discomfort at Sky on Friday afternoon was heightened, but I finished everything they wanted me to do. I didn't want to attend the party because of my position and used the 'jet-lag' excuse to leave for Wellington.

Safely back at home, I devised a blue-print plan. I would keep quiet until Monday, meet David at the airport because nobody would recognise him, sign the contract, and then spend Tuesday telling everybody what I had done - Paul and Pat, Clive Currie, Don Bond, Andy Leslie, Grizz Wyllie, the Union and of course my friends. Only then, would I let the media know.

However, on Saturday, I was just preparing to go out and watch Ories play a club game (I'd cried off with an 'injury') when the 'phone rang. It was Phil Love from the New Zealand Evening Post:

"John, I've heard you'll be signing for Leeds" he said.

"Oh, really, ?" I replied, "Tell me more".

He then proceeded to tell me almost exactly what was going on. I asked him where he had heard the rumours, but he wouldn't tell me (and still hasn't told me to this day).

"Do you have anything to say ?," he asked.

"There's loads of stories going round about lots of players at the moment and I reckon I'm just next in line for it," I said, "Sorry, I can't help you" and put the receiver down.

Blast, I thought, that could ruin everything.

At the Ories game, I saw Don Bond sat on the embankment watching the game and went to sit next to him. After a few moments he turned to me, hair fell over his face and he removed his cigarette:

"Kipper," he said.

"Yes, Bondy," I replied.

"There's this guy from the Evening Post been pestering me. He says you have signed, or are going to sign, to play Rugby League in Britain. But don't worry, I told them it was a load of old rubbish," and he looked away towards the game.

"Bondy," I said solemnly, and he looked back "I'm afraid it's true". He looked away again and then turned back. I could see there was a tear in his eye. I felt as if I had stabbed him in the back, because he had become a bit like a father to me while I was out there. He asked me to tell him more, and I told him the entire story from start to finish. We discussed it briefly and agreed that I should tell Andy Leslie as soon as possible. Unfortunately he was away with his wife and we decided to wait until Sunday.

The next day, we both went round to Andy's house and told him (I had decided that I wanted to tell everybody face-to-face rather than over the 'phone). Although flabbergasted, he was marvellous. Instead of tearing me off a strip, he told me that his father had played soccer professionally in Scotland, and he thought being asked to play any sport professionally was a great honour. He even concluded the same way as Allan Hewson had, saying that he probably would've done the same thing given the opportunity.

Still at Andy's house, I called Clive Currie and he came over with Jill. He was equally as understanding, wished me luck and said he wished he was ten years younger. Next, I tried Pat, Paul and Schuey, but with no luck. All the time I was keeping fingers crossed behind my back that I would be able to contact everybody before the media and, more importantly to me, they would understand why I had decided to switch.

Back at home the 'phone was going non-stop but I had it switched permanently through to the answer-phone. All the calls were from the media wanting to know what was going on and whether I would do an 'exclusive' interview. In the middle of all this confusion my cousin, Tony Hetherton, turned up on my doorstep. He was doing a tour of Australia and New Zealand, and thought he would pay me a quiet visit. I told him, he was very welcome to stay, but not to answer the 'phone or the door and never to say that I was 'in'.

Next thing I knew, on Monday morning, I was having a shower and the 'phone rang. Before the answerphone clicked into action, Tony's heavy footsteps made their way over and I heard him pick up the receiver. "John, it's for yoo-hoo," he bellowed. I came out dripping wet with a towel wrapped round my waist and I mouthed to him, "I'm not blessed-well in, get it into your head". Without putting his hand over the mouth-piece he replied, "Oh yes, I forgot," then he turned back to the 'phone and said, "Sorry, I thought he was in but he isn't" and slammed down the receiver.

Ten seconds later - tap, tap, tap on the front door. By now I was in my bedroom getting changed and I hardly heard it. However, Tony obviously did and he darted over to see who it was. I rushed out to stop him, just in time to hear two press reporters asking if I was around. Tony looked over his left shoulder, saw me dragging my right index finger across my throat, looked back at the reporters, panicked and slammed the door in their face.

Now it was my turn to panic. I threw on the nearest clothes I could find and took a surreptitious look out of one of the upstairs windows. The pressmen were sitting in their car at the top of my drive, blocking my car in and making sure that I couldn't leave. It was such a blatant disregard for my privacy and rights that I got angry. Determined that they wouldn't win, I went back downstairs and 'phoned Coxy:

"Coxy, thank goodness you're there," I said when he answered.

"Kipper," he replied, "What's wrong ?"

"Don't go to out, just stay at your house"

"But, I've got to go to work, Kipper"

"I don't care, be late. Stay at your house," and I put the 'phone down. I then told Tony that I wasn't going to be around for a day or two and to make himself at home. Outside the back of my house was a steep bank covered in gorse bushes and no other houses. Between the bushes ran an intricate mesh of footpaths and bridleways, one of which went for about half a mile, to Coxy's house. I jumped over the fence and made my escape.

As I burst through his door, Coxy was looking really excited and demanded to know what was going on. Breathlessly I explained the story, and said that he should keep ringing up from work to find out the latest. He obviously thought that he was becoming embroiled in some sort of spy-thriller, because he replied with a wink and spun the tyres on his old van as he left for work.

A little later, I managed to get hold of Lindsay to explain that David Ward was expected that evening. He said there wasn't any problem and he'd be round to have a look at the contract for me. By this time, I was beginning to get nervous and wanted someone around, so I called Schuey at his work-place. He wasn't in when I initially got through, but he showed up at mid-day. When he called, I said for him to come over immediately, which he did. I told him the whole story and expected him to be on my side.

"What ?" he said incredulously and I looked at him in surprise. "Thanks a lot," he continued, "what am I going to do now ?". I was utterly speechless at his reaction. After all, he had been approached by many Rugby League clubs in the past and had only narrowly decided to turn them down. I pointed this out to him: "Yeh," he said, "and I only turned them down because I was afraid of what you might say. I suppose I'm going to have to do the same now, aren't I ?"

John was one of the most popular sports personalities in New Zealand where he was often referred to as New Zealand's favourite Pom. His switch to Rugby League came as a major surprise to the whole nation. We would occasionally talk about Rugby League but it never crossed my mind that he would ever leave Rugby Union. His departure to Leeds definitely played a part in my decision to switch codes. I am confident that John will make a big impression in Rugby League as he did in Rugby Union and I can only wish him the very best. Perhaps, and hopefully, at some stage I will have the pleasure of playing with, if not against, him again.
JOHN SCHUSTER

So far, so good. Everybody I had managed to tell had understood my situation, and agreed that I'd done the best thing. That only left the minor fact that I hadn't yet signed the contract and my whole life still stood to be blown away. If things went wrong, my Rugby Union career would be in tatters and my promotions company wouldn't be worth a penny. Those thoughts totally grounded me and I just had to sit in a room, on my own, fighting with numerous visions of the future. There were still a lot of people who I needed to tell, but my nerves were a mess. Apart from Schuey's and the odd excited visit from Coxy, I spent the day reflecting and listening to the news bulletins which, ahead of all the politics and international news, led with the story of my 'signing'.

As the afternoon wore on, I realised that I would no longer be able to meet David at the airport. I tried to explain to Coxy what he looked like but it wasn't going in. However, Coxy gave me the idea to call Mike Kuiti, who was in Wellington and who had already played for Leeds. I did so, and Mike graciously agreed to pick David up.

Meanwhile, Coxy had decided that there might be trouble at the airport (I think he was expecting a shoot-out between the KGB and the CIA or something similar) so he went to get a couple of friends to act as body-guards. Now, Coxy is a big lad anyway, but you should have seen the size of his Rugby League playing Maori mates who turned up on the doorstep. Under strict instructions not to cause any bother, they set off for the airport in Coxy's old, broken-down, white transit van which had a window missing where he had accidentally stuck through a rolled up piece of carpet.

In the arrivals hall at the airport, David was coming through baggage reclaim along with the entire New Zealand under-seventeen Rugby Union team returning from a trip round Australia. As he came through the door he was faced with a barrage of press photographers and three television crews. He knew that the New Zealanders were keen about their rugby, but he thought it was all a bit over the top for a junior team. However, it slowly dawned on him, as he wandered around the arrivals hall, that the cameras were on him and not on the under-seventeens. The reporters converged on him and he told more than one of them, ever so politely, to go away. Another asked him if he was there to sign up John Gallagher, to which he replied "John Who ?". Yet another got pushed out of the way and several expletives were used.

Mike and Coxy came to his aid and helped him outside with his bags. Coxy had said to Mike to follow him, and they would lose the press in the backstreets of Wellington. As the media dived into their cars, Mike screeched up behind Coxy's van in the car park with David in the back to make a quick getaway. Coxy, looked into his mirror and went to zoom off, but stalled the van. It took five minutes turning the engine over before it re-started, and by that time the press had caught up. There followed a wild-goose chase for about fifteen to twenty minutes before they managed to shake off their followers. Back at Coxy's house, I was beginning to worry about their late arrival.

The entourage eventually arrived and I thanked everybody for their help. Not wanting to mess about any longer, we got down to business straight away. David produced the contract, I gave it a quick glance, Lindsay looked it over a bit more closely and at approximately 5:59 p.m. on Monday 21st May 1990, I signed for Leeds Rugby League Football Club. Just as I put pen to paper, Coxy interrupted and asked if he could take a photograph of me signing, I said he could. Unfortunately, he was to find out the next week that he didn't have any film in the camera !

Starting to relax, I put on the television to watch the national news. It started with a view from a helicopter hovering above Wellington. As the camera panned round the sky-line, the commentary said "Somewhere in Wellington this evening, John Gallagher is in hiding. It is believed that later on tonight at this hotel..." and they zoomed in on the hotel we had originally booked David into but managed to change "...John Gallagher will sign for Leeds Rugby League Club".

I had arranged with Bondy that I would go along to Wellington training that evening and tell the team what I had done (it was supposed to be before the media found out). When I got there, the cameras were already in place, but I no longer felt as if I had to hide because I had finally signed the necessary papers. There was no way that I was going to be able to avoid them this time, so I told them that I wanted to have a word with the team and then I would hold an impromptu press-conference.

The players were marvellous and all wished me the best. The last person I came to was Lolani Koko who had returned to the side, he looked me in the eye and said, in his deep Samoan accent, "Oh, Kipper. Bad news, bad news". He had a tear in his eye which made me choke as well.

Back outside, I waited until all the papers and TV channels were represented until I said anything. I definitely didn't want to explain myself time-and-time again, and I didn't want anybody left out in case it prompted them to speculate with some untrue rubbish - I was going to get enough flak anyway.

Next day, Tuesday, I belatedly set about calling everybody I had wanted to speak to before the news broke, including Grizz, Pat, Paul and Eddie. A few of them were understandably hurt that they had first heard the news on the TV, but the unanimous verdict was that I'd taken the right option. Grizz even said that he would have done the same thing if he had been given the chance, just like Andy Leslie and Clive Currie had said.

On Wednesday I flew to England and on up to Leeds for the 'official' press-conference. It wasn't until then that I realised my news had kept the naming of the soccer World Cup squad off the back pages of some tabloids in England. I really was surprised and pleased at how much interest was being shown by my 'home' country. One thing that did disturb me was the immediate equating of my name with success at the club. A number of reporters asked me if I thought my signing would bring an end to the drought of trophies at Leeds. I answered that I hadn't even played the game yet, so how was I to know. But deep down, I thought they were getting a little ahead of themselves in their search for a shocking headline. Of course, they were only beginning the first part of their quaint custom by building me up, so they could knock me down later.

Apparently John didn't receive my letter before he came back to England. While he was hiding in Wellington I was sitting at home hoping for a 'phone call. It never came and I felt really down hearted, John must have got my letter and changed his mind or decided again that he couldn't make any commitments. In the end I asked my Mum if I could use her 'phone to call John and see what his thoughts were. She understood what I was feeling and gave me permission.

Because I didn't know John's number in New Zealand, I had to call his home in Ladywell to ask his mother what it was. When I got through, she surprised me by telling me that John was actually in England. Naturally, I asked if he could call me back and sat down to wait again.

That same evening he called and explained that he'd just signed for Leeds and that he was coming over here to live. The news didn't really surprise me and didn't make any difference because I already knew we were going to end up together. Call it intuition or whatever, I could just tell that this time we were going to make a success of our relationship. All John's signing had done was speed things up and save me a lot of money in air fares.

ANITA

Having hardly set foot in England, I was back on the plane to New Zealand to sort everything out. I spent a frantic week trying to arrange for the shipment of all my things and the sale of my house while saying endless goodbyes. I was helped in the latter by Ories who put on a fantastic leaving party for me, to which nearly three hundred people turned up. Just about all my friends were there, including Grizz who came along with Eddie Tonks, Chairman of the New Zealand Rugby Union, in a very nice gesture. In a way, I found it all very sad.

Also upsetting was saying goodbye to a little friend I'd had for a couple of years. While walking out of my local gym in 1988, I'd spotted a crowd near the entrance. When I'd pushed through to see what was going on, there was a lovely little puppy about a month old with big bright eyes, floppy ears and huge pads on his feet. The gym's manager, Joe, was a friend of mine and he'd said the dog was a stray which had wandered in off the street a couple of hours previously. I'd stayed a while, having a milk shake and playing with the puppy.

Before long I'd noticed that everybody else had gone apart from Joe, myself and the dog. I'd asked him what he was going to do with it and he'd said he didn't know. He'd called the RSPCA but nobody had reported it missing. I'd thought it would be great to have such a lovely dog keep me company for a few weeks. So I'd taken it home, given my number to the RSPCA and scanned the local papers to see if anybody reported it missing. Even if the owners did turn up, I'd have a new pal for a short time.

No one had ever claimed it and he became my constant companion, growing-up into a cross between a labrador and a spaniel. However his puppy-like temperament never left him and he constantly dug up my garden, messed up the house, chewed my pine rocking-chair, pinched the neighbours milk, came back with kid's dolls, and buried my washing in the flower beds. The back of the house resembled a bomb-site, but I liked him. His colouring was a mixture between black and tan, so I'd settled on the name 'Guinness Gallagher'.

Guinness was really a New Zealand dog and loved roaming round the suburbs so there is no way I wanted to bring him over to England. When I told everybody I was going, there was no end of people unwilling to take such a house-wrecker. However, while I was away in England for the press conference, my flatmates called up the local radio station and asked if anybody wanted John Gallagher's dog ! A big American friend called Fred Sawaya, who took the Wellington side for conditioning, heard it and volunteered. Guinness subsequently moved across town from the eastern suburbs and is probably terrorising the southern suburbs right now.

Chapter 16

Kicking-off at Leeds

My third trip half-way round the world in as many weeks left me feeling very tired, so I had a couple of days to recover in London before driving up to Leeds. It was nice to sit back and relax for a change, and it gave me a chance to see more of Anita. When I did drive up to Leeds, I did so on my own. Leeds was easy to find and so was Headingley, but it took me about three-quarters of an hour to find the club on St Michael's Lane, which is a little back-street. At the club, I was met by Alf who took me to a small temporary flat in Alwoodley, north Leeds, where I was to stay until I found a house.

Five minutes inside the door, I had just started to unpack when the 'phone rang. I was surprised and thought 'Boy, that was quick'. As I picked it up, I heard a Welsh accent on the other end say, "Kipper, is that you ?". I was really taken aback because I didn't know that anybody in the UK knew my nickname. It turned out to be one of the Leeds players, Phil Ford, who I'd briefly met in an Australian lift. He said that he and a few of the other players were about to go out and celebrate centre David Creaser's birthday. I wouldn't have dreamed of anything other than accepting.

The celebrations turned out to be taking place in Wakefield, quite a way from Leeds, but it was worth the trip. Apart from them knowing a bar which was serving pints for only ten pence, it served to break the ice between me and them. I'd been worried that all the hype surrounding my signing and supposed record-fee would serve to isolate me from the rest of the players. But none of them took any notice of it apart from in fun. I had a great evening and began to realise I was going to enjoy living 'up north'. Next morning I woke up with a tremendous headache and I remember thinking 'so this is professional Rugby League - it's just like Rugby Union really !'.

The first few training sessions involved heavy weights in a nearby gym. I got to meet the rest of the team, who were just as friendly as the 'birthday' mob, and started to shake some of the rust out of my system. One of the problems I was facing was the fact that I had joined Leeds in the middle of the New Zealand season. Stepping back up to pre-season training from mid-season fitness needed a lot of effort, and it didn't help that I'd done virtually nothing with all my rushing about. In July we started back outside with some sprints at the local Carnegie sports college. I still remembered the advice Tony O'Malley had given me on my departure for Ories, and put everything into working as hard as possible.

I hadn't realised how close Carnegie was and I started to investigate what courses were available. To start with, I thought I'd like to do something such as Sports Physiotherapy with a view to setting up a small practice when I retired. But my enquiries revealed that all the courses were very intensive, and the college didn't want to take in anybody who had been outside studying for a long period. The course I finally decided on was Human Movement, one step down from Physiotherapy. A contact at the club managed to get me an interview and I was duly offered a place as an 'overseas student' to start in September. I was told I would have to pay my own fees, as I'd expected, which wasn't going to leave me much after paying a mortgage and buying food. However, I saw it as an investment, so I accepted their offer.

My relationship with Anita was also developing and she came up to visit nearly every week-end. Before long we'd realised that we were made for each other, to coin a cliché. Anita left her job in London and moved up to Leeds where she has settled in and found new employment.

Religiously, every Friday, I caught the 6:03 p.m. train from Kings Cross which got into Leeds at 8:40 p.m. where John would pick me up. We would then spend the week-end together before I'd leave on the Sunday lunchtime. If I'd stayed to watch John playing rugby, then I'd have got into London very late and in the dark which I didn't want to do. My credit card took a hammering and it was another financial relief when I moved up to be with him.
ANITA

The season, for me, started on 12th August in a friendly match against the nearby second division club of Bramley. There was a big build-up in the press, and the game was a testimonial for two of the Bramley players, Peter Lister and Paul Fletcher, but only about four thousand people turned up. Leeds were never going to be threatened, so a mixture of first team and second team players were named in the squad along with a couple of new faces such as myself. I knew the chances of my getting on the pitch were going to be good because, as a friendly, there was no limit on the number of substitutes that could be used. However, I was picked by David to start the game.

Speaking to him before the game he told me that he knew I could kick, and that I was the second choice kicker for the All Blacks (behind Grant Fox but ahead of Frano Botica). However, he had wanted to keep some of the pressure off me, and since there were plenty of people who had kicked for the team before he would only call on me if I was needed. Instead, Simon Irving, who was stepping up from the second team, took all the kicks and continued to do a good job for most of the season.

My usual nerves returned and, as I jogged out onto the pitch, I just wanted to get stuck in as quickly as possible. It wasn't to be, and the first ten minutes were fairly quiet with me not being required to do much. Then scrum-half Paul Harkin spotted me and threw out a wide pass, which I sent straight on to winger Warren Wilson who scorched down the touchline for a try. That gave me a bit of encouragement, because we had scored the first try and I had played a part in it.

Not long after, I was hanging behind the winger, John Bentley, about thirty five metres out from the line. As the ball came out, I spotted a gap over his shoulder, so I sprinted for it and called for the ball. John gave a nice flip-up for me to grab and get through the defensive hole. From there it was a short run to the line and my first Rugby League try. Naturally I was relieved and pleased that I'd started well. Just about everyone in the team came over to shake my hand.

I must admit that I wasn't really understanding what was going on in front of me, it being my first game of League. Fortunately the Leeds forwards were dominating Bramley which meant there was a good supply of ball. Since I hadn't got the hang of forward play, I spent most of the attacks trying to link in with the back-line and playing the sort of game I knew. Also, Rob Ackerman, another

Union convert, was playing at centre and he called me into the line a few times when I was lost. In defence, I didn't have too much to do. There were a few high bombs put up for me and on the first of them I was taken out about a minute before the ball came down. We got a penalty and I remember thinking that I wouldn't like to experience such a hit too often. Little did I know that it was going to continue all season !

At half-time, David Ward asked me how I was feeling. I replied that I was fine and he put me back on for the second half. Almost immediately I found myself receiving a pass from Rob, drawing the cover and putting another new player, Eddie Rombo from Kenya, away for a run and eventual try. Five minutes later, David pulled me off and put on a substitute. As I came off he had a big smile on his face and said, "That was a good start, well done". I was more than happy; I'd not done anything wrong, I'd had a hand in three tries and I'd scored one myself. That night, I slept well.

We had another friendly against a second division side, Ryedale-York, before the 'competitive season' started in earnest. York proved to be a lot stronger side to Bramley but we had our international players in Garry Schofield, Carl Gibson and Roy Powell back in the side after their successful tour with Great Britain to Papua New Guinea and New Zealand. We won by 42-6, and again I got my name on the scoresheet, taking an inside pass from Carl a few metres in front of the line.

David kept me on for the full eighty minutes, and the ground was wet which pulled at my legs. When those factors were combined with a generally higher pace during the game, I ended up feeling fairly tired. It didn't surprise me because a lot of people had said I would find Rugby League more tiring than Rugby Union, because of its higher tempo and the ball being in play for longer periods. However, I was to find out that the 'real thing' was up yet another gear.

Bradford is the closest big city to Leeds and their side, Bradford Northern, fall into the traditional category of 'local rivals'. I was told that we could expect to play Bradford at least three times during the season, since the teams were always being drawn together in knockout competitions. They were correct, and we were drawn to play them at home in the first round of the Yorkshire Cup (The Yorkshire and Lancashire Cups are knockout competitions which are always played at the start of a new season). Adding to the excitement was the line-up of transferred players. The Leeds team which was named for the game contained two ex-Northern players, whilst theirs contained two ex-Leeds.

David tried to keep a lot of the media attention away from me but it was nigh-on impossible. I was getting telephone calls to the flat and all sorts. In the end, I decided on a policy of openness; they were going to 'get' me somehow or somewhere, so I chose to make myself available at times and places convenient to me. A lot of the press boys don't realise how much they can mess up your personal life. They might think that one call at an unreasonable hour isn't too bad but, when multiplied several times over, it becomes a pain. They also don't pay much respect to ones feelings; when a reporter, newspaper or magazine publishes several scathing articles about me, they still express surprise when I say I don't want to talk to them.

Match day was blessed by glorious sunshine with a large crowd of approximately fourteen thousand turning up to watch. When I got out of the car at the club, I was immediately faced with a TV crew from British Satellite Broadcasting, who wanted to know if Leeds were going to win the championship now they had signed me ! Safely in the changing rooms, my nerves returned and I started to warm up with everybody else.

It struck me at that moment how similar everything was to the amateur code; even though everybody was being paid to be there, the general atmosphere was exactly the same. The only difference I noticed from being an All Black was the depth of back-up. I had been used to there being a substitute, just as good as me, waiting to take my place, with somebody in line behind him and one behind him, etc. Here, there was only the second team to rely on. Financial restrictions in League mean there is usually only one specialist substitute for any position and subsequent replacements have to be drawn from different areas. There just aren't as many feeder systems as there are in Union. I hadn't realised how 'small' such a 'big' club was.

Just before kick-off time we went out for a warm-up on the Headingley cricket ground. This really surprised me because I'd assumed it to be hallowed turf and didn't think anybody was allowed on it, especially rugby players. But we kept to the outside boundary and only did a few strides and a bit of stretching. Going back into the changing rooms, I saw Dad, Pat and Kieran who'd come up to watch the game. Even though I was deep in concentration, their calls of good-luck broke through the background noise and I acknowledged them.

Out on the pitch I began to get even more nervous and just wanted to get started. When we did, I learnt straight away we were in a local derby; the speed, the physical confrontation and the atmosphere were totally different to those friendly games. Bradford got it together almost from kick-off and put us under a lot of pressure while we were still trying to find our feet. Within minutes they had taken the lead through one of their Leeds-old-boys, Paul Medley, who shrugged off two tackles to score. Northern continued to attack ferociously for the next quarter of an hour and we had to pull out all the stops in defence.

On one occasion, when we were trying to run the ball out of our own twenty-two, I received a short pass from one of our forwards near the centre of the pitch. Just as it came to hand, I was hit like a ton of bricks by two of Bradford's forwards, Karl Fairbank and Paul Medley. They really took the stuffing out of me and I was seeing stars as I stood up to play-the-ball. It was the first of many such tackles that I would receive during the season.

Our scoreline deficit was eased a little when Simon Irving kicked a penalty, but this was wiped out minutes later by a penalty against us. Slowly but surely our forwards started getting back in the game and holding their own in mid-field. This led to us closing the score down to 6-8 with a try by Phil Ford. I had a slight hand in the move, but it was really the simple transfer of a pass than anything else.

When the half-time hooter went, I think we were counting ourselves fortunate to only be trailing by two points. David was non-too pleased, and rightly so, because the team wasn't gelling at all. Everybody was making mistakes which was putting unwanted strain on our defence.

In the second half we came out a lot stronger and Bradford looked as if they were tiring. A few minutes had passed when the ball was kicked deep by Bradford on their fourth tackle. Our wingers had dropped back and John Bentley fielded the ball. He then put a wide pass out to me as the cover closed-in around him. I could see the main Bradford line bearing down on me, but I could also see that they weren't coming up straight. I managed to run round the first man and cut inside the second before he could adjust and come across. That left me free to make a break past four or five players and I took the ball about thirty-five metres up to the half-way line. There, I flicked the ball out to one of the props, Paul Dixon, who carried the move on before off-loading the ball to Paul Harkin. The little scrum-half made a bit of headway before passing to Fordy, who was surrounded by the regrouping defence and found himself with nowhere to go. He performed about five side-steps on the spot, a bit like a dazzled rabbit in headlights, totally confusing the opposition plus the rest of his teammates as well ! Eventually, Mike Kuiti came up on his outside and took the ball down the touchline. Fordy stayed in support and took the inside pass, when Mike was tackled, to dive over for his second try. It was converted and we hit the front for the first time in the game.

Further effort from our forwards saw us pressuring the Bradford line again. This was when stand-off and captain, Garry Schofield, showed his experience and abilities, to take a tap penalty just in front of the Bradford try-line and nip over for a touchdown. At 16-8, and with only twenty minutes to go, we were looking good to progress into the quarter-final. Unfortunately, Bradford refused to give in and were stung into action. They took the game by the scruff of the neck and put in three tries plus two conversions to win by 16-24. On two of the tries I found myself face-to-face with a rampaging opposition forward; the first one ran through my tackle as if I wasn't there, while I managed to bring down the second one he got his pass away before hitting the ground.

Back in the changing rooms I was totally overcome by tiredness. The game had been played at a fast and furious pace throughout and, on such a hot day, my reserves of energy had been depleted. Nevertheless, I'd thoroughly enjoyed it and knew that League was going to provide me with the new challenge I'd been seeking. The game was a lot more physical and I was going to need to be a lot stronger.

The loss was a bitter pill to swallow because I was very aware of being on trial due to the media attention. After the game, I had to attend a press conference along with David Ward and Garry Schofield. They asked me how I'd found my first game, to which I replied, "Bloody hard !". David was then asked if he was disappointed at losing the match having signed me, and I was asked how it felt to be on a losing side for the first time. Having completed their first stage of building us up in the off-season, the press were now entering their favourite pastime of chopping us back down. David reminded them that there was plenty of the season left to go, and I pointed out how many times I had lost with Ories and Wellington. They were only looking at my international record and totally forgetting that I'd played domestic rugby as well.

We were to lose again two weeks later when the first division championship started. We travelled over the M62 motorway to the Watersheddings for our opening game against newly promoted Oldham. Just about everybody thought we would come away with two points, but we were frustrated by a very determined home side. As a team, we played a lot better than we had against Bradford but again we let it slip in the last twenty minutes to lose 22-32. It didn't help that we had Paul Harkin sent off for tripping, which was later rescinded by the disciplinary committee, and had to play all the second half with only twelve men.

During the match, I'd concentrated on not making any mistakes and polishing up my defence. Mostly, I succeeded and put in quite a few good tackles in the second half including the last twenty minutes. Unfortunately the Oldham backs always seemed to support the break, and somebody was usually on hand to take the late pass when I committed myself.

The bad run continued into our third game, and first championship fixture at Headingley, against Hull. Yet again we found ourselves in the lead, this time by 22-14, with twenty minutes to go. And yet again we let it slip, with Paul Harkin sin-binned again through no fault of his own, to lose by 22-24.

The frustrating thing was the team had been playing well. With the Bradford game excepted, we should have been winning but were failing at the death. David even got us together and told us as much, saying that he was happy with our performances against Oldham and Hull and that a win wasn't far round the corner. Personally, I was happy with the way I'd started my new career. After each game I'd taken a long look at the statistics board to see if I was lacking in any department. While I wasn't excelling in any field, I wasn't falling behind either, and my stats were comparable with the team's as a whole.

Chapter 17

A Different Ball Game

Our first win came in our fourth match, against Warrington, at Wilderspool. This time the team managed to click for the whole eighty minutes instead of collapsing at the end and we ran out winners by 22-10. There was a huge sigh of relief after the match as if the heavy weight of expectation had finally been lifted from our shoulders. Back in Leeds, we ended up celebrating into the small hours what were to be the first points in a good run.

To make things even better I scored my first 'real' try. We were points up, 12-4, when Paul Dixon ran off Paul Harkin's shoulder, to break four attempted tackles and come within three metres of the line. I followed him on the way in, just in case, and when he realised that he wasn't going to make it, he slipped me a pass and I dived over for the touchdown. It was a great feeling and all the players came over to congratulate me.

Having the need to win and gain two league points every week wasn't new to me, because I'd been used to a similar set-up in New Zealand. The only difference as far as I could see, between Union in New Zealand and League in Britain with respect to winning or losing, was the monetary factor. In both codes, I'd found totally dedicated sides desperate to win and maintain a good position in their respective leagues or divisions. But what makes it fractionally harder for the professional player to face in defeat is the lack of a winning bonus. There is quite a large difference between what you take home after a victory compared to a loss. For turning up and playing in a losing side, you are paid about £60, whilst a winning bonus will boost that sum up to around £250 (this is the same for everybody in the team which is important). I think most players want to win anyway and the extra pay is a nicety but it does add another dimension to the result.

The game of League itself is very different in just about every aspect to Union. Other than in the basic principles of rugby, like having to carry an oval ball over the opposition's try-line to score, the two codes are distinctive:

The defensive lines in Union may be up to five deep with different players covering various 'depths' on their own side. With there being so many stoppages in play, and therefore plenty of time for defences to regroup, a breakthrough from broken play is relatively uncommon. The mid-field is always very tight and most breaks will come down the flanks where an overlap is created. As a full-back, these are easier to cover because you can see which side the play is heading towards and position yourself respectively. If the opposition does come through, then you can always use the sideline to angle him out of play, or force him to change direction and come inside where the backmost defensive line should have repositioned.

In League, on the other hand, the team all move up in one line making it very difficult to breakthrough anywhere. However, if the opposition does make a break, there are usually no other lines of defence in front of the full-back. The run may come down the touchline where you can use the same tactics as in Union, but it may equally come down the centre giving the attacking player lots of room in which to move.

In Union it is sufficient to do your homework and find out when a stand-off is likely to kick, plus which foot he'll use. By watching him closely and seeing how he is positioned on the field it is relatively easy to tell when, and to where, he is going to put the ball. In League you need to constantly keep track of the number of tackles, which you just don't do in Union, as well as watching where players are standing. There may also be more than one player in a League team capable of kicking the ball forward or kicking for touch, which makes it a lot harder to anticipate and position yourself accordingly. Not knowing the opposition players as well as I did in Union, I have to rely a lot on teamsheets and videos provided by the Leeds coaching staff.

Tackling as a full-back in Rugby League is also very different from Rugby Union. Whereas I may have been required to make only one or two tackles a game in Union, I'm required to make twelve to fifteen in League. The tackle itself in Union depends very much on who is coming at you. Firstly, they are unlikely to be coming straight towards you as in League, and secondly their physical shapes vary a lot more. When faced with a towering lock-forward in Union I always went straight for his legs, which is the weak point of a tall person, knowing that he would have to release the ball when he hit the ground and that my defensive lines would be close at hand. If a smaller player such as a winger or scrum-half broke through, then I would usually attempt to smother him and the ball by tackling around the arms and chest.

In League, the players all seem to be of a more similar height and build; much stockier and stronger in their upper-body. This type of player is very hard to bring down, especially since they will be well trained in staying on their feet until they can release the ball. I've found the only answer as an individual is to hit them harder, and I've had to step up my weight training to make me capable of bringing more players down. Obviously, its important in League to get as many players into the tackle as possible, with somebody going in low and another up high.

As a full-back in Union, I had a lot more options when taking a high ball than I currently have in League. Firstly, there was always the possibility of taking a 'mark' in my own twenty-two in the amateur code, which doesn't exist in the professional game. Secondly, I am usually confronted by an on-rushing wall of opposition players in the thirteen-a-side version, giving me no option but to run straight at them, while looking for a possible weak link in the circle. When taking a high ball in the fifteen-a-side version, I could usually count on a bit more support from my loose-forwards, because they would have been closer to me when the ball was kicked. In League the line is trying to push up as far as possible so the forwards have further to come back. This also makes it more difficult for me when I'm being pressured as I go for the ball. With a deeper defence in Union, I could count on a couple of forwards shielding me from the incoming attack. In League I'm more exposed and likely to get hit harder.

There are differences too in the various other positions. A Rugby Union prop would find that he'd need to shed one to two stones to make the grade in League. Where he would probably be a bit stronger and more useful in power situations, such as scrummaging, he wouldn't have the mobility required in League. I'm not saying the Union props are unfit, but they would need more insurance in their legs. Conversely, a League prop moving into Union would need to add some weight to make himself more powerful in the scrummaging and rucking situations where a lot of pushing, shoving and pulling goes on. Although, under the present rules, no League player can move into Union (with the exception of France ?), I think it is important to contemplate the possibility. Its more usual only to consider a Union player switching to League, but if players from the two codes are to be compared then you must think about both directions.

International locks are often over six-feet five-inches tall, and are honed into taking the line-out ball. They are more like basket ball players than anything else, and would probably have more chance on court than they would in Rugby League. I think their sheer height would also make them more prone to injury, though the strength and mobility of players such as Gary Whetton and Murray Pierce would be in their favour. To a degree, in Union, a good big one will often beat a good little one, but in League a low centre of gravity is almost as important as size. Virtually no Rugby League second-rower would make it into Union, at a comparative level, because of the need for height.

The loose-forward positions are probably the closest of all amongst the big men. A switch in either direction would be on the cards due to the resemblance of their games, especially between number thirteen in Rugby League and open-side flanker in Rugby Union. Both have to be able to run all day, tackle all day, use their strength in the scrums and support the ball. Obviously, I've never played the position in either code and don't know the finer points, but I feel the similarity of skills required make them easier positions in which to swap.

A hooker in Rugby Union is almost like a fourth loose-forward, making a switch into League very plausible. The actual hooking role in scrums is more refined in Union but open field play is similar. Of course the League hooker looking to move into Union would also have to learn a whole new area of play with line-outs.

The very specialist position of scrum-half initially looks alike in both codes. These players need to be bubbly, jinky, low centre of gravity players with good kicking skills and a good pass. However, the positional play and understanding of the two games is very different. In essence, they are applying the same skills to dissimilar games and need to be in different places at different times. Given plenty of time to learn new rules and lots of playing experience, I don't see why a good scrum-half shouldn't be able to successfully change codes. But I think they will need to be very patient.

The same goes for Stand-off; two of the best players to come into League, Jonathan Davies and Frano Botica, have both found it difficult to make their initial impressions in the number-six shirt. This position requires a fundamental understanding of the game, in whichever style of rugby, to make their playing decisions almost second nature. Again, with the games being so different to play, their correct choice in one code would probably be the wrong option in the other.

The centre and wing positions are the obvious ones for players to make a quick and successful swap between codes. On both sides of the fence, Wingers are essentially there to score tries with a few defensive duties, and don't often have to think too much about passing options. Perhaps a League winger will have to make more tackles and therefore be stronger than a Union winger, but basically they are the same in both codes. The centre is one of the more attractive positions to play whichever way you look at it. Again, the only major difference I can see is in the number of tackles that are needed.

Learning the new rules is an obvious and necessary step to anyone making the switch. This is an area where anybody coming from Union to League would have the advantage over a player going the other way. If the respective rule-books were to be laid side-by-side, I think the Union version would be about ten times thicker than the League version. This explains why Union is so stop-start and it is a definite plus in favour of Rugby League.

The difference in scrums and the lack of line-outs in League must be responsible for a lot of the discrepancy. Scrummaging in Union is almost an art-form with all the different ways that the ball can come out. The same can not be said of Rugby League where it is purely a means of restarting play in various situations. Interpretation of the scrummaging rules by referees in either code can have a large bearing on the game. In Union, it almost always comes down to the personality of the particular referee in charge, and the packs very quickly learn what they can do with each one. In League, some referees take more notice of infringements than others. There are a lot less rules to be broken, but some referees don't even seem to care about the ones which do exist. In both codes I think there is a need for the ruling bodies to get together and make the application of rules more consistent.

The ball always comes out of Rugby Union scrums a lot cleaner, through one of the myriad of tunnels, than it does in Rugby League. In the professional version, the ball can, and usually does, come out any old way. That makes the League scrums look very disorganised and almost a farce, but it does get the ball back into play a lot quicker. The Union version always causes a lot of messing about and the ball can be lost for minutes on end, which gives League a huge advantage as a spectacle for the casual onlooker.

Obviously, a comparison can't be made when it comes to line-outs. Suffice is to say, I once met a referee who told me that he could find a penalty in every line-out that has ever been played !

Which brings me to the subject of penalties. When a penalty is taken in League, the ball can go out on-the-full and the team awarded the penalty retains possession. With this not being the case in Union, and with there being three points for a goal, almost as many as for a try, attempts at the sticks are a lot more common in Union. Because of its importance, more Union players practice their field-kicking a lot more, and I think it is fair to say that Union kickers are generally more accurate than their League counterparts.

Kicking during the course of play is a very different proposition because of the different rules. Almost anytime a Union player receives the ball in his own twenty-two he will kick it out. Of course, he can do this in the knowledge that it can go straight out and it doesn't make any difference. This also makes Union less attractive to the casual spectator because it prevents the long periods of intense attacking pressure which are common in League.

Adapting to all these differences has been quite taxing. One of the main things I've altered is my weight; putting on about half a stone since I left New Zealand. However, there is still a long way to go on this score and I want to bulk up lot more in the close-season. It will help me in several respects, making me stronger and less prone to injury. The Rugby League season is a long one on the body and my frame needs all the natural protection it can get. In my first year I felt strong and fit right up to January, then the hits started to have more effect ending up with me getting injured a couple of times.

The added strength will also help me hand people off and keep on my feet as long as possible when held.

While I'm learning the new game, I'm still using the same thought patterns as I did in Union. I still weigh up who are the strongest players in each side, and what might be the best patterns to run against them. I haven't thought too much about protecting myself in the harsher tackles. If I did this, then I would start thinking about getting hurt or injured, and I would start to hesitate. Instead, I've adopted the philosophy of just going and doing what's required. It might not be the most intelligent way of approaching the problem, but it has worked for me.

I think the majority of my adaptation to the new game will come from experience and the abilities of my teammates. As in all great teams, from the Liverpool soccer side to the Wigan Rugby League outfit, players benefit from staying together as a unit. The team at Leeds has been a bit unsettled, but hopefully now it will become more stable and I'll be able to grow with it. The current All Black side is very similar to the one which won the 1987 World Cup, and the few new players in the side have come up to the required level quicker because of their integration into a stable, skilful team.

Off the pitch, it has been every easy to integrate. It is commonly thought in Union circles that there is no social life associated with League. Whilst this is right in some respects, it is wrong in others; professional League players don't go out drinking every night but they do socialise regularly. Compared to a small Union club side, it will look as if the League players hardly ever go out, but this is because they are professionals and have a job of work to do on the pitch. If they went out too much, they wouldn't play to their highest standard and would soon find themselves without a 'job'. Rugby has to come high up on the priority list. On the other hand, they do socialise in the same way as any set of people who work together normally do, just like office workers in a way. It should also be noted that this type of behaviour isn't the sole property of the professional League player; those wanting to achieve a high level in the amateur code can't afford to spend too many nights on the town.

There's always a lot of controversy about which is the better game and which side would win a contest between the two - Union or League. On the subject of which is 'better', I can say without any doubt that they are both great games and we should leave it at that. As to which side would win a match between the two, it depends on which rules are to be played. The RFL recently proposed a game of two halves, one under Union rules and one under League rules, in aid of charity. Well, obviously the Union team would win under their rules and the League team under theirs.

The League boys wouldn't stand a chance under Union rules because they wouldn't win any line-out ball and probably not much from the scrums either. The game amongst the backs would probably be fairly even with the League side being very physical. That would probably lead to a lot of penalties against them, to add to the ones they'd pick up from forgetting to release the ball when tackled. I think there would also be a few scuffles if one of the League players took a ball and got trampled on by a set of huge onrushing Union props.

In the half under League rules it would be the opposite story. The Union props and locks would find it tough keeping up with the pace of the game and the League side would find itself with lots of room to operate. Certainly the amateur's calves would all be turning to jelly after ten minutes with all the retreating five metres to get onside. The play-the-ball itself would confuse most of the Union players and every single one of them would forget to count the tackles. In summary, both sides would get a hiding in one half and make it back in the other. Final score ? 40-40.

Perhaps a better question to ask is 'which is the more attractive to the spectator ?', since both codes need backsides on seats to survive. This is where I think Rugby League has a slight edge on Rugby Union. The professional code is undoubtedly more interesting to someone who has never watched a game of rugby before and, indeed, to some of those who have. The reason for that is the greater pace of the game and the fewer breaks in play. However, somebody who is used to watching or playing Rugby Union can find a lot more going on in tactics of the fifteen-a-side game, and therefore derive a great deal of pleasure from a match which a lot of un-informed people would call boring. Anybody who 'knocks' either game should really try to be a bit more constructive and look for the good points; they are two different games. Perhaps, if a few people from Union got off their high-horses and a few people from League took the chips off their shoulders, then there could be a new harmony in the great game of Rugby. It would be sad to think that there is going to be another hundred years of bickering.

Chapter 18

Making Progress

The win at Warrington sparked off a revival in Leeds' fortunes, and we followed it up with a good win under floodlights against St Helens at home. I managed to pick up another try which made me happy. To add to my delight, there were four of my old All Black colleagues, who had come over for the Barbarians centenary celebrations, in the stands watching the game. After that, we gained revenge with a comfortable win over Bradford in the league at their ground, but had a bit of a hiccup against Featherstone due to a refereeing error in the final minutes.

While we were coming together, the all-powerful Australian tourists had arrived and were annihilating everybody they played. On the same day we were losing to Featherstone, they were trampling all over the Champions and Challenge Cup holders, Wigan, by 34-6 at Central Park. As a result, and with our rather erratic form, nobody really held out much hope for us in our game against the tourists just seven days later.

The day of the game day was beautiful with a bit of a wind, which suited me down to the ground being used to windy Wellington. They were fielding a near test-strength side, and we put out our strongest team in an effort to avoid a humiliating defeat, as had happened the previous time Australia visited Headingley. One of the major battles of the game was going to be between the stand-offs; we had the probable Great Britain number-six in Garry Schofield while they were playing their likely test candidate, Laurie Daley. The confrontation turned out to be intriguing with Garry matching Laurie for strength and power but probably getting the edge in creativity. As a result we were able to stand up to the Kangaroos in a way which no other side had to date.

After about fifteen minutes, Garry took the ball from acting half-back at the play-the-ball and ran on the blind side. As he did so, I saw a gap between one of the Aussie centres and the loose-forward. Running at an angle, I called for the ball and he gave me a lovely delayed pass, to put me through before I knew it. I was able to cut inside the cover with an arching run, and sprint for the right hand corner out of the full-back's reach. As I touched down there was a huge roar and we went four points up.

Only eight minutes later Paul Dixon arrived first under a high kick from Garry to score our second try. Simon managed to add the goal and we took a very surprising 10-0 lead. For the rest of the first-half we were probably the better team on the field and had a few opportunities to stretch our advantage. However, we lost the ball in a tackle just before half-time and they scored to make it 10-6 at the break.

In the second half, we held our own and gave them a real fright. I made a couple of breaks and Simon Irving came close to taking a wide-open interception. The crowd really got behind us and we tried to pace our game, knowing they would come back strongly near the end. Unfortunately that's just what they did and hit the front with another try after nearly fifty minutes. With their pack taking an increasing command, it perhaps isn't surprising that they grabbed another two tries in the last five minutes to win by 10-22. They all looked very relieved as they walked off after the final hooter, and I think the scoreline flattered them.

Running the tourists so close suddenly gave the Great Britain camp a new lease of life. Up until then, it had all been doom and gloom and most people were expecting a 3-0 victory in the test series to the Australians. However, our performance showed that they could be challenged. The selectors obviously agreed and chose Garry, Paul Dixon, Roy Powell and Carl Gibson for the test squad. Of course, history shows that they were right to be optimistic and Great Britain went on to win the first test at Wembley in spectacular fashion.

The press were also taking notice of my fairly good start to the season and, in particular, the try I scored against the Kangaroos. Several of them were tipping me for a place in the Great Britain squad which I thought was very premature, considering I'd only been playing the game a few months. Their enthusiasm led to a lot of 'phone calls asking me which team I would play for - Great Britain or New Zealand. I still have to prove myself, but given the chance, I would opt for Great Britain. The reasons for this are, yet again, ones of practicality. I've started my studies at college and I wouldn't be able to play for New Zealand without missing large chunks of my course. Since I class my education as very important for the future, I wouldn't want to do that. If, however, I'd completed my studies by the time I'm honoured by international selection, then it would probably be a case of 'first come, first served'.

Things continued to go well for myself and Leeds until the end of the year. Over Christmas and the New Year we were faced with a busy fixture programme:

First up on 16th December we played Sheffield at the new Don Valley Stadium, and had Simon Irving sent off for an alleged trip while we were points up. Sheffield then came at us strongly and almost levelled the scores. With about twenty minutes left to go, they put together a very useful attack and looked certain to score with a two-man overlap, when the floodlights went out. We all went back to the changing rooms, and David Ward warned the officials that we would cool down and face injury if the delay was longer than fifteen minutes. Fourteen-and-a-half minutes later the lights came on and we resumed the game. Fortunately for us, Sheffield had cooled down more than we had, and we notched up three more tries to win. It was nice to have a bit of luck go our way for a change.

The following week we played against Wigan, who'd started the season slowly. They also took their time to get going against us and we were leading for the majority of the first half, before they scored a couple of late tries. In the second half they really whitewashed us, but I scored a couple of tries and felt that my form was progressing very well.

Next up was our third game against rivals Bradford, on Boxing Day. We won again, this time fairly comfortably 26-8, in some of the worst conditions I've ever played in. The sleet was pelting horizontally across the pitch, and the icy wind must have been gusting around forty miles-an-hour. It was the spectators who deserved the applause, rather than the players, because they had to stand still in it all. At one point I looked up to see the floodlights swaying for several metres from side-to-side.

On New Years Day we played Oldham at Headingley, also in bitterly cold conditions. Some slack tackling gave them a twelve point start but we came back to win 28-12. I picked up a try and was given my first man-of-the-match award. Apart from being happy at the award itself, I saw it as a great start to the New Year and a good omen for the coming months.

Up until this point of the season I'd been happy with the progress I'd been making in my new sport. True, I hadn't set the professional code alight, but I hadn't expected to. Most of what I've ever achieved has come through persistence and hard work over a couple of years. Unfortunately it was really the highest point I was going to reach. A series of injuries, incidents and bad luck were to mar the remainder of my season.

The first one came in our game against Hull, the week after playing Oldham. The game was played at Hull's ground and it was to be their last game with Brian Smith in charge. Since he had been a guru at the club for several years, they were going to beat anybody that night. We lost 14-34, but with fifteen minutes to go, I went up for a high-ball and was taken out by an incoming forward with it still three metres above my head. To make matters worse, he hit me with his knee up and I fell awkwardly which forced me leave the field with a thigh injury.

I had to miss the next game and made my comeback the week after, against St Helens. We had a good first half but went in at the break trailing by a slender two points, 6-8. Early in the second half, one of the Saints forwards grubber-kicked the ball through our defence into my arms, just two or three metres short of our line. I took a few steps sideways and then went to accept the tackle of two players bearing down on me. As I went down, I felt one of them grab me round the waist while the other got hold of my ankles, pushed them together and lifted them into the air. At one point I was suspended with my feet directly above me and my head about thirty centimetres above the ground. There was nothing I could do about it because I had hold of the ball and didn't want to leave go. I was then pile-driven into the dirt with quite a force which wrenched my neck. The noise was similar to the one your knees sometimes make if you stand up too quickly, and everything went numb. I held onto the ball for what I thought was a few seconds, and then assumed the referee had seen what happened, so let go. However, the ref called a fair tackle and awarded a scrum to St Helens from which they scored.

The first thing I did was feel my hands and toes because I couldn't move my neck. All the team were stood around me and eventually the physio arrived. He made a few more checks, and then helped me get to my feet when a bit of feeling returned. I was slowly helped off the pitch, and then taken straight to the hospital for some X-rays. The diagnosis said that my neck had been badly wrenched but no permanent damage had been done, so I was free to go home.

After the Hull game, I'd called home to let Mum know I was alright in case she had seen it on TV and was worrying about me. It turned out that she hadn't even known it was going to be on. Me calling her made her start worrying, whereas she hadn't been before. Therefore, I didn't bother calling home with my latest injury, even though it was potentially very dangerous, since there hadn't been any national TV cameras at the game. Twenty-four hours later, Mum rang up in a panic; one of my cousins in New Zealand had rung her, saying she had just seen me being spear-tackled on the news and was I OK !

The club had made a video of the incident, and they sent it to the Rugby Football League pointing out the seriousness of the incident. After looking at it a few times, the RFL agreed that it was a spear-tackle so they made several copies and sent them out to all referees.

One of the not-so-smart decisions I made during the season was to make an immediate return into the side against Warrington. I'd thought my neck was fine during training, but in the middle of the match it started hurting again, and I spent the rest of the game worrying rather than watching what was happening on the pitch. I also declared myself fit for the following week to play against second division Dewsbury in the first round of the Challenge Cup. Just as I was regaining my confidence, the same spear-tackle trick was tried on me again. Luckily for me, this time they didn't have enough strength to turn me right over and the resulting pain wasn't as bad as it could have been. The distribution of the video obviously hadn't reached every referee.

Then, in the second round of the Cup (against Bradford, again), I picked up a knee injury late in the game. That injury put me out of action for another couple of weeks. I don't know if all the injuries would have happened anyway, but I was beginning to feel as if my body had taken enough for one year. I took a long look at my training diaries and came to the conclusion that I was going to need to 'bulk up' even more in the coming close-season.

With all the injuries and the knocks to my confidence, my game went off the boil and I started to become a bit stale. It also coincided with a stagnation in the club's fortunes; following our good run in November/December we'd taken a dive in form and dropped several places in the division. Our final match saw us lose again to Wigan, by 8-20, as they re-claimed the Division One Championship. We'd faced them at the end of a week in which they had to play four tough games, but they were still too strong for us. In my opinion they thoroughly deserved to take the top honours.

We finished in fifth place which put us into the Premiership Trophy for the top eight clubs. We were disappointed not to have finished higher and it meant that we were surrendering home advantage to the fourth placed side (in the Premiership; first plays eighth, second plays seventh, etc). Having been knocked out in the first round of the Yorkshire Cup, the second round of the Regal Trophy, the second round of the Challenge Cup and not winning the first division, we were looking at a fruitless year despite all the pre-season hype. Our final chance was at the Premiership, so we stepped up our efforts.

It seemed to work in the first round against Castleford and we scored in the final minute to win a tight match. That put us into the second round, and semi-final, against Hull. We played out another tight game, and it looked as if we were going to win 7-4, with a few minutes left. Our forwards were tackling out of their skin. Then, with two minutes to go, a high-ball was put up in my direction. It came down near to where I was standing, about two metres from our line, and I jumped up sideways to minimise the chances of a knock-on if I dropped it. As I stretched my arms out, I was hit by two of Hull's players who were coming-in at speed and also jumping for the ball. With their forward motion and me virtually jumping from standing-still, I was knocked backwards and I didn't get my hands to the ball. As we fell to the floor, it bobbled around and unfortunately a Hull hand was first to touch it down. With such little time left, we couldn't come-back and went out 7-10. I've viewed the video several times, but I still can't see what else I could have done. Everybody was disappointed, but all the players recognised that I'd had the ball knocked from my grasp. Nevertheless, it was discouraging to be involved with the incident which ended our season.

I spent a lot of the summer concentrating fairly heavily on passing my first year exams at college. This time I didn't have any 'laurels' to rest on and I made sure that I put in a lot of hours revising. Behind Rugby League, I now put studying as my second priority and anything else, such as TV work or promotional appearances, have to take their place.

However, there is one part of my life which takes priority over everything else and always will, including rugby and studying. That is, of course, my time with Anita. I finally plucked up the courage to propose to her, and on 3rd August 1991 we got married.

The rest of the time, I spent looking at my strong points and my weak points. Yet again, I concluded my poor form in the second half of the season stemmed from not having that extra bit of bulk to protect my frame. I resolved to do lots more 'heavy' weights and even invested in a small bench which I put in my garage. At the same time, Doug Laughton from Widnes replaced David Ward as coach, and he told the press that he was going to 'build me up'. All the talk of more muscle prompted speculation in the media that I was going to become another Arnold Schwarzenegger !

I've taken a lot of flak since I changed codes, as expected. My standing in Rugby Union, and the reported size of my signing fee, have made me a natural target for criticism. However, I've gone through a really steep learning curve and I believe I've got what it takes. The rugby world hasn't heard the last of John Gallagher, just yet.